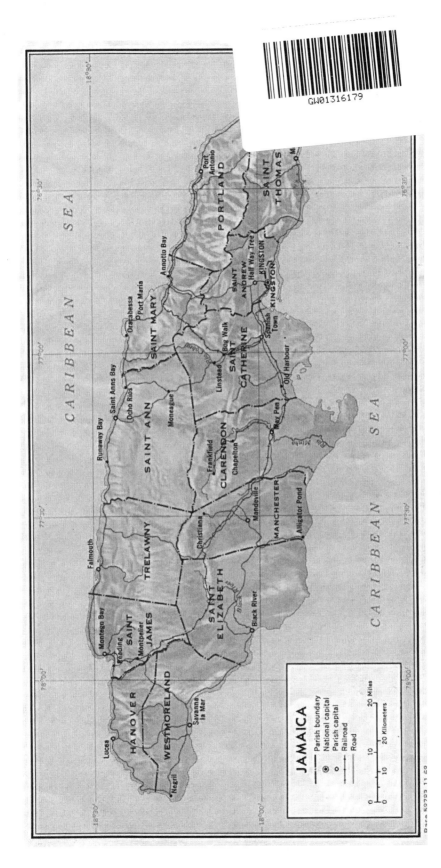

A Jamaican Childhood

Beverly Icilyn Ramsay

Acknowledgements

I wish to thank my daughter Zara Nortley who has listened to many of these stories throughout her childhood and has encouraged me to begin my writing journey, to Sally-Anne Fawcett, herself an author of some repute, and her husband Anthony Wendt, who have both given of their precious time in the perusal of the manuscript.

Thanks also to Christine Coombes who for years has encouraged me to commit my stories to paper, to Charlotte Knowland and Sheila Nortley who have found time in their busy lives to closely read revised copies of my manuscript, and to the many friends and relatives too numerous to mention, who have supported me through occasional periods of flagging enthusiasm for my craft. My thanks also to Tina Skilton for her excellent editing skills and her invaluable advice which served to move me closer to my goal of publication.

Thanks is also extended to Sarah Dixon who not only prepared the manuscript for publication, but also created the fabulous book cover which I feel not only conjures up the flavour of the text beautifully, but also gives an accurate representation of the cheerful, cheeky child the narrator would have been many decades ago!

Dedication

This book is dedicated to my wonderful daughter Zara Nortley, my late father Alton Ramsay who fostered in me a great love of words, and also to my late grandparents Olga and Sam Walker, without whose love and care these memories would not have been created... or retained!

Great experiences creates great memories...

My grandmother Mrs O Walker, in 1977   Mr. Sam Walker with one of his American Fishtail cars!

Copyright © 2018

Beverly Icilyn Ramsay

All rights reserved.

ISBN-13: 978-1984034700

ISBN-10: 1984034707

Contents

The Big Sky 11

School's Out 19

The Worldlians 31

Gold 43

Puppies Are Coming 61

Bad Man 81

Introduction

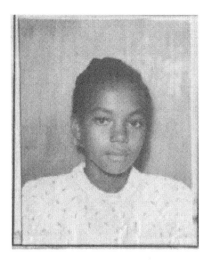

A Jamaican Childhood is set between the mid 1950's and early 1960's; a time when many individuals and families from the Caribbean were immigrating on the invitation of the British Government, to help with the rebuilding of England after the 2nd World war, and also to improve their own lives.

The introductory narrative sets the scene of the environment in which the narrator grew up, while the stories are recollections of events which took place in her life from age four to eleven when she lived with her grandparents, after her parents and older sibling had left for England.

The Big Sky

When you're a young child living on a never ending swathe of land, surrounded by all the flora and fauna anyone could ever dream of, every day is full of wonder, excitement, adventure, and sometimes even drama!

Pleasant Farm was a huge sprawl of land in the parish of St. Annes, which sat on a vast plateau from which I gained a three-hundred-and sixty-degrees view of the surrounding villages and large colourful houses dotted about in the lush variegated green landscape. Our farm, or rather my grandparents Sam and Olga Walker's farm, comprised of banana plantations, orange groves, coconut and pimento walks, coffee groves, cow pastures and chicken runs, enclosed on one side by a clear, swiftflowing river which splashed by on its way to the sea in Ocho Rios, while the Gale Road and the Content Road curved around us on the remaining sides. My grandparents had, decades before I was born, discovered and cleared this large tract of land and converted it from what was known as an abandoned wilderness into the model farm it had become. But without the people living in the surrounding villages and hamlets, all of the developments would not have been possible.

The story goes that the workers, all men, came daily to tend the livestock, chop trees, reap harvests and replenish the soil, while the women came to help my grandmother with the cooking, the washing and ironing and maybe even general companionship when my grandad, Mass Sam as the workers called him, went off on his daily journey in his brightly coloured fishtail car, to Tower Isles where he conducted his business. When I came to live with them, after my parents had left for England 'to help the Mother Country', children, offspring of visitors, usually came to play at weekends to prevent me, according to my grandmother, "from having too much of big people's company". Play would entail having a tour and survey of the animals, chasing chickens and dogs games, or just sitting and pretending to be invisible while the adults laughed and talked.

One important visitor was my brother Ludlow who lived in Ocho Rios with my aunt and uncle. His visits were the highpoint of my life and for each of these, I prepared weeks in advance, the activities to which I would introduce him. The games we would play, the things I needed to show him and the fruits I wanted him to taste. Playing my big sister role was to be taken to supreme elevation, and all he needed to do was to be my little brother and just acknowledge my superior knowledge by fawning over all the preparations that I had made for his enjoyment.

When there were no visitors, only the radio intervened in our lives on many of those dark evenings as we sat on the veranda reading, talking and looking out into the darkness of the land. This magical contraption, this talking box, was all gold and mahogany and it had pride of place on an elaborately covered table which stood forever in one corner of the drawing room. Never could this table be removed or shaken because on the outside wall adjacent to it but out of sight, stood the tallest most deep rooted aerial post which was said to be the bearer of news, plays and broadcast from anywhere in the world. This to me was pure magic and on many occasions when it was switched on and instantly produced the sound of music or news from around the world, I could be found surreptitiously creeping round the table to take a sneaky look through the holes which peppered the board at the back. I yearned to see the small people inside who had come down from Kingston or even over from America or England. After one of my investigations I had been let off with a warning that 'yu going to spoil yu eye' and the table had been pushed closer to the wall at an awkward angle impossible for a seven-year-old to navigate.

One of the benefits of my grandad's Tower Isles taxi business which ferried overseas tourists around our island, was that through the forgetfulness of his customers, a whole stream of books came into my possession.

Shakespeare's 'A Midsummer Night's Dream', 'Don Quixote', and 'Lorna Doone' to name but a few, were devoured voraciously by me, and although I failed to understand each story in its entirety, my vocabulary and imagination were greatly enriched as plots slowly unfolded. But now they did not occur in distant lands where the authors had set them, but in familiar locations around the farm and along my route to school or church.

For 'A Midsummer Night's Dream', my imagination sought out a distant cool glade in the cow pastures for the most magical of scene, while the antics of 'Don Quixote' and 'Sancho Panza' took shape on a bare patch of ground which lay just outside the kitchen window, while the Doone's hideout was in a dark, damp, tree infested location along the Content Road. Interestingly enough, I later gathered, from a film version of 'Lorna Doone' that my imagined setting had been spot on!

One person who paid us regular visits was my favourite relative, Aunt Hermin. She was probably a teenager so still had a lot of fun in her, and together we played rough and tumble games, and chasing. She was also my confidante and saviour when the grownups were out of sorts, but there was an unseen boundary which I crossed at my peril. Silently she demanded for herself, the respect due to an older person. Any aberration of her expectation would result in a stern look or even a smack around the legs; but on the whole we got on like sisters. I loved her and believed everything she told me, without question. It was through aunt Hermin that I received a very valuable piece of information which kept me occupied and guessing from the time I arrived at Pleasant Farm, age four.

One night, when I was staring quizzically up at the sparkly surface of the sky, she revealed to me that the shape in the moon was that of an actual old man. She stared unblinkingly into my eyes and added that if I looked hard enough I would see him eat the cheese that he lived on for his breakfast lunch and dinner. I continued to look very hard at the shape and, yes…yes…yes! I could definitely see the seated figure of an old man holding what undeniably appeared to be a large chunk of Jamaican cheese pointing towards his open mouth. But as hard as I stared I could not see him biting or chewing the delicious cheese. My desire to detect any motion on his part kept me interested, entranced and occupied for at least another two or three years.

In a bid to see this fantastic action, it was not unusual for me to suddenly leap up from the veranda, rush through the connecting rooms to take a glance at the big shiny moon which hung suspended over the house. But after some time I decided that maybe creeping up to spy on the man in the moon would be more productive as I came to the conclusion that he only ate cheese when he wasn't being watched. So I would silently creep up to a corner of the house by the radio pole, and peep around. But still no luck. No matter what tactics I employed, I always found him only preparing to bite his cheese.

He certainly gained my respect for being able to sit in one place for so long and only live on cheese and nothing else.

Years later, all my beliefs, and awe and wonder were swiftly shattered in an instant when I told one of my uncles of my wish to catch the man in the moon eating cheese. His reply of 'Stap talk foolishness bout man in de moon!' followed by a loud kissing of his teeth with a hiss which sounded as if a whole heap of freshly seasoned mutton had been flung into boiling hot oil. After his explosion of disgust, his lips settled into an unpleasant curl, and in that instant I developed a lifetime dislike of him for shattering my dream.

Another relative, my youngest and nicest, Uncle Willy, entertained me in more robust games. He would, after firmly clutching my hands, spin me around at a great speed which caused my legs to rise from the ground and throw my whole body into a petrified star shape. The speed of movement caused the world to spin furiously and trees, sky, dogs and chickens would merge into a kaleidoscopic blur. Then he would set me down and release me; at which point everything began to whirl at breakneck speed, and the usually placid sky would toss and turn and tilt and lurch wildly in many directions. Time after time, on being set back on the ground, I would try desperately to steady my weakened legs to keep myself upright. But on most occasions they gave way beneath me, so I was forced to sit patiently where I had fallen and wait for the whole world to stop spinning; only to be whirled around again!

The sky was an important part of our lives and it seemed to offer support to my grandmother. So many answers to her questions seemed to be gleaned from this big sky. For example, if she wanted to know what sort of day or night it was going to be, she looked up at the sky and commented obscurely on the colour, the shape of clouds and whether they were moving or stable. Whenever she had a knotty problem to solve she seemed to look up at the sky for a solution. Often her eyes looked troubled when she looked up but seemed calm when they descended. She would roll her eyes up to the sky in a strange fashion if she was cross with me, especially when I asked a lot of questions; and sometimes, when I supposed the sky did not produce a satisfactory answer, she would tell me in a voice which sounded slightly dangerous, to go and find a task to do, to maybe read a book, or to water the flowers; in fact, to do anything which took me out of her sight for the moment. And I never waited to be told twice.

The sky above us also served as the flight path for aeroplanes. Whenever one flew overhead, my gran would calmly turn her beautiful round face upwards and announce its country of origin. If it was England she would follow its trail of smoke wistfully and I would know that she was thinking of her daughter – my mum.

She could also tell by looking at that expanse of blue if our chickens were in danger as she observed the slow wafting kite-like circling of hawks over our farm. Once their purpose was ascertained, I was quite happy to drive them away with shouts and whoops or even by throwing a few stones which never hit the threatening target but made me feel that I was saving the life of a chicken or guinea fowl.

The sky was also our natural weatherforecaster. At the start of a blazingly hot day we would sometimes see on the far horizon in the district of Gale, a sudden block of whiteness that seemed to grow larger by the second and had the look of a swiftly marching and determined army intent on destruction. In spite of having seen this spectacle on countless occasions I would stand rooted to the spot in open mouthed wonder until I heard the warning screech 'Rain, Rain' shouted either by my gran, my aunt or our helper, Miss Vie. Then suddenly, like the police bursting out from hiding to catch a culprit, all the ladies would dart towards the washing line, scattering dogs, cats, chickens and slow children. I knew the drill, and would hold my skirt out for the pegs while all hands wildly flung sheets, underwear, night clothes, grandad's many check trousers, my cousin Errol's pastel coloured shirts, my grandma's billowing dresses and undergarments, together with several flowery tablecloths, into the huge two-handled wicker basket. We would, as usual, finish not a moment too soon as just after the shout of 'Run!', huge silver raindrops, like water-filled balloons, would splash down as we made our escape into the nearest bedroom, panting, laughing and folding warm clothes with satisfaction.

While the grownups acknowledged their good fortune at getting the washing in on time, I would look out of the window in wonder as the dry earth became sodden and the leaves of the trees waved in happiness at receiving this sudden thirst-quenching downpour; all of which was swallowed up minutes later by blazing sunshine issuing down from a now, surprisingly bright blue sky.

It was within or close to this landscape that events contained in this book, took place.

Happy reading!

School's Out!

The big boys were in a category of their very own. These were boys who in age and size had out-grown not just their classmates but also their uniforms, the school furniture, and even forms of acceptable school behaviour. And why were they still in school, you may ask. Because year after desperate year they were recalled to study for and resit the impossible demands of the final exam. The one they kept failing. The one, if they were successful at it, would show the world that school had not been a waste of time and according to the teachers, "Government money".

So, yoked to the organisation like huge tethered animals baying for freedom, they had to their credit, desperately sought through copious amounts of head scratchings and deep soul-searching sighs, to find answers to things they had never been taught, methods that had never been shown and problems they had no idea existed until they had confronted them looming like frightening and gigantic puzzles, written up in an unknown language, in the examination room. So, they grew bigger and older in the system while being provoked, challenged and thwarted again and again by interminable and unfathomable tests and exams.

But contrary to their thinking, the flaw was not in them but in the outdated mechanics of the organisation that kept these helpless over-grown boys, and occasionally a girl, tied to an institution which they had physically and mentally outgrown. In an environment where they were not only the tallest but as evidenced by the bulkiness of their structure, the oldest.

So, each September saw the return of these students; taller, older and stockier, reluctantly ascending the threshold of The Flaxhill All Age School. And sometimes in the distance one could see a mother with arms folded and bearing a stern and challenging expression, watching the slow progress of their big offspring making his way, far too slowly, far too reluctantly, up the steps, at the top of which stood Mr Wilson the head teacher, bearing a wry smile on his honey coloured face. Often, he greeted them with their name and in a surprised voice, said 'So yu back wid us again?' And the returnee would mumble his assent followed by an audible 'Sir' while his legs suggested distinctly that he might be on the verge of collapse, or might even be considering turning tail and running - past his mother - for the not too distant hills. But they never did. Not then anyway. Maybe later as pressure rose or tempers flared, or pride rose up and saw the futility of their situation and so claimed back self-respect after an encounter with a long-hated teacher harbouring sadistic tendencies. But not today with his mother looking on. And probably holding a belt.

Now to the majority of the school population, these overgrown boys were nice and polite. Some were willing breakers of almonds for small girls, opener of doors for nice teachers, and sought-after teller of good stories about the many methods by which they outwitted their hapless parents. However, even some of these good people, as time and time again failure whittled away their personalities, often became scowling, growling, and dissatisfied individuals - the bane of everyone's life. Of anxious parents, of teachers, and sometimes of children of already nervous dispositions who haphazardly stumbled into their paths.

Imprisoned daily by small and restrictive chairs designed for pupils half their size and age, an air of permanent embarrassment etched on their faces but dressed up as bravado and displayed in a couldn't care less attitude, they sat, towering above the much younger children. Day after day they tried valiantly to engage with and decipher the contents of books positioned, because of their height and the need to share, at a distance from their straining eyes. Once more for them, the ensuing frustration of engaging with the printed word, which lay lifeless before them only added to their daily struggles of surviving in a physically and mentally repressive regime.

So over time, the frustration became compounded by the accumulation of days, of jeers and veiled insults. Humiliation became indelibly stamped across their defiant faces and in their slightly braced shoulders. To glance, or worse stare, in their directions inside or outside of the safety of the sometimes-gladiatorial atmosphere of the classroom, was to court trouble. To accidentally wander into their vicinity and even worse, to brush against their bristling person created a response in the unwitting rambler to that of touching a live electrical wire; a wire raw and waiting to engage and sting. Angry scowls found a permanent home on many of their haunted faces already stamped with the scars and scratches of battles fought and battles possibly won.

These were dangerous boys.

Excluded from the society of men, amongst whom many rightly belonged, they found delight instead in taunting weaker boys within the school population. Younger more successful boys, with heads down and bent on winning a successful future to make the daily grind worthwhile, were often to be seen skirting past them wrapped in cloaks of invisibility and just out of arms reach. And even some teachers were not exempt from the wrath of some of these boys. The really brave or reckless ones, harassed and confused for too many hours by the printed word, developed and presented a challenging body-stance or two, or even a short and quiet kiss-teeth, while the very bold, mad or just stir-crazy, occasionally threw down verbal challenges to their elders and betters.

Now, the whole population the length and breadth of the island of Jamaica would have preferred to jump into a pit of ravenous lions rather than challenge a teacher. Least of all the sort of teacher whose message to their new class at the start of each new term included the information in their introductory speech that "Anyone in hiear who tink dem is bad man mus know dat dey looking deth in the feace".

In fact one such teacher, who we all believed must have been practicing his craft for at least a hundred years, was given the nickname of 'Deth in de Feace'. And another, after an incident which saw the shirt of an escaping recalcitrant torn from his back, became secretly known as 'Dethman'.

The nickname was an open secret between children and the said teacher, and like all Jamaican bearers of these names that summarised an aspect of their personalities, he secretly revelled in his claim to fame. So soon after the alias became entrenched, one new and uninitiated student, the first of many, was encouraged by his over-helpful classmates to address the teacher with that said moniker, preceded by 'Mr'. He was of course completely taken by surprise at the furious response of the teacher, who in a booming voice demanded of his terrified pupil 'Where yu get that from bwoy?' as if he himself had no knowledge of his own nickname. The victim, looking for assistance from his new comrades found only a wilderness of slightly shaking shoulders and serious faces boring steadfastly into exercise books. Some upside down.

On the subject of sadistic teachers, many parents while sitting on lamp-lit verandas and staring out into the darkness liberally punctuated by the incessant winking lights of peenie wallies, narrated to their children, blood curdling stories of teachers in their schooldays who had ruled their pupils, good and bad, with a rod of iron. They gave accounts of pitched classroom battles brought on in their opinion, by teachers who were mad with their own importance, and they confirmed that back then, these had always happened, as they did now, in the hottest part of the afternoon. At a time when the classroom clock tick-tocked the countdown to the cessation of the school day, when frivolous freedom beckoned through the open door, and the aromas of evening meals being prepared in the surrounding homes, wafted in through the half-opened windows.

It was during one of those times that the overgrown boy had taken the decision to be the main character in his own blockbuster.

After the first vocal shots had been fired, the reluctant onlookers and bit players, had looked on with shock, trepidation and a good deal of anticipation and alarm. In an atmosphere charged with impending violence, the audience had automatically put on their protective armour of elbows pressed into sides as if to hold in bated breaths, while with slightly bent heads they had stared with unseeing eyes at opened exercise books. As the atmosphere thickened with danger, their frightened fingers held their rigid unmoving pencils and they waited for the inevitable clash. They had witnessed these dramas before and knew how it would end. The big boy would be grabbed ahead of his dash for freedom, pinned into his desk before he had untangled himself from restrictive and inanimate wooden legs. A frantic message for help would be relayed to the headmaster via a winged-feet student messenger otherwise known as 'teacher's pet', who would sprint quickly away, spurred on partly out of relief at escaping the battle ground and partly from happiness to be the bearer of bad news and the opportunity to be a part of a story that would undoubtedly have an unhappy ending. The audience could predict that once the message had been delivered, they would then just wait for the drama to unfold and move sharply into Act two with the sudden and terrible arrival of the avenging head teacher. Without a struggle but with a vice-like grip, one that would include not just khaki shirt but also large amounts of flesh and possibly bone, the culprit would be restrained by the head teacher until such time as it took the captive to acknowledge the error of his ways which was usually evident in less audible breathing, a cessation of struggling, and a lack of expletives.

Now his fellow pupils, all much younger and more prone to feelings of sorrow and sympathy, would watch as the next not unfamiliar scene unfolded. Wide eyed and concerned they looked on as their friend, the offender who had dared to challenge a teacher - this purveyor of all knowledge and successful futures and a king or queen amongst mere mortals – was unceremoniously hauled off. Now engaged afresh in a new variety of struggles which were accompanied by noisy recanting of his deeds, he was led away to the head teachers study - known to all pupils as 'The Lion's Den'. Then all would wait for the sudden silence to descend and for the sounds of the inevitable thwacks of the merciless cane which would come just before the highpitched wail of the unfortunate chancer. But as familiar as the children were with the ending of such dramas, they were also familiar with variations on that theme.

They knew that on emerging from The Den, some unfortunates would return contrite and subdued, quite the opposite to the manner in which they had left the classroom. Too busy now soothing stinging hands with puffs of cool air since they had not unfortunately had a chance to be protected from damage by the magical antiseptic qualities of the leaves of the kuritch bush. Nor had they had a chance to surreptitiously massage the same potion into their now pulsating nether regions. These same cushions of flesh which on occasion also had the added security of an exercise book or two, pressed into double service as an armour against the onslaught of a rapidly applied cane. So now, duly chastened, they would try to settle back in their seats, albeit in a somewhat over-rehearsed, lopsided, some may say, laid-back position.

But some of the exits made from the confinements of the head's study were not so demure and conciliatory. Those students also known as 'The RBB's (The Real Bad Boys) would, after their thrashing, often reappear from the swiftly yanked-open door like a bullet from a newly-fired gun - their roars suggesting to all and sundry that the brutal chastisement had been ineffectual and had not had the desired effect of subduing them, but had instead created in the victim a now colossal amount of resentment and rage. Their rapid movements among and on top of the serried rows of peopled-desks, coupled with guttural sounding expletives, indicated plainly that they had no intention of re-joining their studious peers and were instead bound for the freedom of the great outdoors. With not even a pause of indecision or backward glance at their former world, they would, with shirt tails flying and arms outstretched like an out of control helicopter, take a death-defying leap down the six rather steep steps, and fly off into the distance as their quite audible forbidden language was carried back on the wings of the afternoon breeze. Their final action of eschewing the opening mechanism of the genteel waisthigh gate and instead leaping over the dangerous points of the picket fence, somehow signalled to all that they were on a journey of no return.

But in the current scenario where a challenge had been made to the teacher's supremacy, there was no running for help or grabbing and taking of a boy. There was just silence. Now the children watched as the teacher, dressed in regulation white short sleeved blouse and black fitted skirt, signalled her intentions by positioning her black leather-shod feet in what could only be described as a gun-slinging posture while she slowly narrowed her blazing eyes in the direction of the boy who in his boldness and foolhardiness combined, had dared to question her authority. The colisseum throbbed with silence, and she, the terminator, the high priestess, fully armed with all her God-given disdain bequeathed to Jamaican teachers in their lofty unassailable heights, locked her glittering eyes full of bullets onto the boy. Poised for action like a snake surveying its prey, she examined him slowly from head to foot. Then in a voice palpating with venom, she drawled

'Bwoy,' and after the slightest of pause as she held his confused gaze, she continued, her tone deep and menacing, 'Yu think yu bad?' Now something invaded the room and the jury without moving their bodies, shifted their eyes to the soon to be demolished accused who sat there, a creature apart - changed, transformed and shrivelled, damaged and already fallen. The boy who for a few seconds had held their secret admiration when he had made his daring challenge, now sat cornered and as good as beaten. They could sense it. They knew that when his answer arrived it would be too late and that it would not hold the magic ingredient by which he could be saved. But he was not even granted the opportunity to deliver his answer. He and they now knew through the slow confident blink of the teacher's eyes that her question had been purely rhetorical. The curl of her upper lip obliterated any doubt and told him that she could not, would not, wait any longer. If she had waited at all. So, with a wry lopsided smirk, she delivered the killer blow. 'Yu jus smell bad!' she said.

Now in a country where cleanliness is valued above all else and is next to Godliness, her words ricocheted around the room and left her audience shaken and breathless. The insult shook them to the core. The pupils and the damaged boy, wide eyed at the audacity and power of her words, prepared themselves for the end that was to come. With a sardonic yet slightly quizzical expression on her face, the teacher, standing in the same Wild West mode, arms folded and legs wide apart, waited for the boy's response while a victory smile slowly spread across her smooth mahogany coloured face and revealed a small portion of her upper teeth, giving her the appearance of an animal about to devour its helpless prey. They all waited for the final move of the demolished boy.

And without warning, it came!

An explosion smashed the silence, and pandemonium erupted in the vicinity of the humiliated victim. Like a mortally wounded animal seeking his escape from the hunter, he burst out from his ill-fitting desk and chair like a maggot too large for its host, and catapulted himself to the centre of the arena. We watched in awe as his sinews strained against his tight-fitting shirt and he suddenly seemed like something that had been pressed down, restricted, restrained forever, but was now free. Bellowing rebelliously like a captured cow sighting the butcher and spurred on with the sudden realisation of an innate will to survive, he moved with superhuman speed towards the far recesses of the room. The instinct to live galvanised his locomotion and caused him to leave in his wake, the remains of upended desks and inkwells, scattered books, kicked over chairs – some still holding on to their surprised occupants - as he grunted and squealed while making his frenzied and desperate journey towards the beckoning sunlit exit of the classroom.

Because of the suddenness of the event, there had been a break with protocol and so the restraining ordered had not been requested. But there was a final obstacle, specially designed for such eventualities. This contraption was the last bastion of security designed to thwart previous, future and present pupils in their desperate bid for freedom. This was a row of desks, securely interlocked and occupied by large, sturdy, heavy children, and had in the past proved too much for desperate escapees, who had wilted and thrown in the towel at the sight of this seemingly insurmountable barricade. Many had stood beaten and weeping in the face of thwarted dreams of freedom and had been forced back by the sudden rough and victorious hands of determined teachers who may have missed their vocation as army sergeant majors; many of those teachers had been peers of the parents of current pupils and known to have been major bullies in playground affairs.

But nothing could stand in the way of this boy. Not today. With eyes wild and full of fire, visibly pulsating muscles and the glow of victory already coursing through his veins, he now displayed a flashing set of bared teeth through which he growled and bellowed with even greater ferocity as he took drastic action in a final bid to thwart his jailers. To break his educational fetters. Devoid of any regard or niceties towards the occupants of this bulwark of security, he braced himself and leapt wildly from desk to desk on shoeless and dirt hardened feet, scattering books and startled backward-bracing children, in his wake. Amid howls and cries of "Miss!"

'Miss!'

'Ooow!'

'Lawd Gad!' from the leapt-on and wounded, he fearlessly charged with what seemed now to be even greater urgency and momentum, towards the promised land. Then finally reaching the exit of freedom, he, with chest braced and biceps flexed, plunged forward with superhuman velocity into the open air as if he alone spied the finishing line held taut and waiting for his victory.

And it was noted by his onlookers, who later narrated the episode, that his charge towards freedom and the promised land, was accomplished with such force, such desperation, and such urgency, that even the escapee had just for a moment, paused in mid-flight to take a quick puzzled glance over his shoulders as though in anticipation of the expected outstretched arm pursuit of the head teacher. But even his audience knew that if reinforcements were summoned, his speed and numerous avenues of escape would have prevented any possibility of his capture.

Now the teacher with no acknowledgement of the earth-shattering event that had occurred, and with victory writ large in her eyes, spoke in a mild and honey-laden voice as if she had had the best of days, 'Children,' she smiled, 'write today's date in your exercise books please'.

In the calmness of the warm afternoon, all that reminded us of the tumultuous event was the now empty and forlorn overturned chair and desk combination in which the boy, our friend, had sat, and on the blackboard, the date which was slowly revealed by the noise of the grating chalk. Thursday October 12, 1961.

The End

The Worldians

When the letter informing her that I too would be leaving for the Mother country, my grandmother Mrs. O. Walker of Pleasant Farm, skimmed one more time, the pages of the airmail letter with the red, white and blue chevron stripes, and then walked swiftly and urgently, without any warning, towards her bedroom door.

Following her unexpectedly exit, after what was usually a welcome missive from 'foreign', my grandfather, noting my gaze said 'Yu granmadda have a headache Cassie. She gone to lie down, so yu can keep your granfadda company.'

In a strangely choked voice the next morning, she uttered some unexpected words. 'Cassie, your parents ready for you an your bradder to come to England, so I haf to take you to say goodbye to your dad's people in Breadnut Hill.'

I was now as surprised as she must have been yesterday on reading those words.

'Send for me, grandma?'

I had no idea I was going to be sent for to go anywhere.

This was my home. As if I hadn't spoken, she continued.

'Dey will want to see you before you travel to England.'

I was always happy to see my numerous cousins and their lovely dads who were brothers of my own dad, but it didn't soften the blow of being sent for. And the following day, soon after the cock crowed and before the heat rose, we set off on our journey which finally brought us to the long Fern Gully Road.

As we strolled past an imposing white church surrounded by a velvet lawn and well-manicured shrubs, a lady, who was tending some flowers and was probably the same age as my grandmother, straightened up from her kneeling position and called out 'Mistress and Walker? How-de-do mam!'. She strolled hurriedly towards us and without pausing for a response, she continued "Is yo granddata dis mam?" while she busily wiped her hands on the flower- patterned apron tied firmly around her middle, she held me in her gaze with half an eye, as she continued, 'Bwoy is long time me no si you Mrs O! Yu looking good mam' she said smiling broadly and revealing a set of teeth packed so tightly together that they appeared eager to make a hasty escape from her overcrowded mouth. Still smiling, she slowly examined my grandmother admiringly from head to foot before returning her full gaze to me. Closely scrutinising my face while her voice adopted a squeaky sing-song tone I recognised as being specially reserved for speaking to small children, she exclaimed

'An who is dis pretty likkle girl?' But before I can formulate my name she answers her own question and directs it to my grandmother. 'Yu gran data?'

My gran grabs a rare pause and replies in her calm voice 'Yes my dear Miss P she says, this is Cassie. Albert and Elisa's second daughter.'

Suddenly, in a higher pitch which alarmed me and a nearby flock of birds, Miss P exclaimed wide eyed 'Dis is Cassie? Yu mean Cassie who her granmadda deliva only de adda day? Goodness gracious!' she screeched. Then the statement all grownups use, 'My! How she grow big. A rememba when she was bawn. Har fadda did help to deliva har, no so?'

'Mam?' exclaims my grandma, using a well-used response

and tone amongst women, designed to indicate agreement.

While my gran and I stand and listen Miss G tries to conduct a roll call of my father's relatives 'Yes, yes bradda Buttley an Hastley and what the odder wan name on de odda side a Fern Gully? A know the wife well. Lovely woman. She pauses, Yes...his name... Alman. And dey did have a sista? Yes; and not for the first time, she answered her own question "A did know har. Lynette! Nice pretty lady. Live in America?' she concludes as she looks off into the distance at something I cannot see.

'Yes, says my gran, And Alston and my daughter in England.'

Ignoring the names provided, Miss P continues

'So what bring you ova to dis side Mrs O?'

'My dauta an her husband sending for she and her brotha.'

'Oh!' she exclaims wide-eyed. 'Dey goin to Hingland!'

'Yes my dear.' my grandma responds solemnly.

Then while Miss G stares at me intently as though a map of The Mother Country is printed on my face, my gran in a surprisingly upbeat voice asks

'So how is your family Miss G?'

The conversation unexpectedly veers towards serious topics like marriages and babies, and I search frantically for an escape. Much better to find something than to be directed to one in disgrace, in the event of being caught 'listening to big people's business'. Finding a diversion or render oneself suddenly deaf and dumb if not invisible when questioned about how much one has heard, were the actions required of children who suddenly found themselves stranded alone in adult company. The rule was that children should not have any knowledge of anything, show any interest or understanding of anything, ask any questions about anything, give any opinions or laugh at any jokes regarding adult issues such as having babies, marriage or bodily functions.

The adult world was a minefield. Not only should children not know anything about childbirth - even that children are born from a woman - but on no account should they reveal that they could recognise when a baby had taken up residence in a lady's tummy. Women were just fat. Yes. Suddenly. Even though their arms and legs remained stick thin? Yes. Any remote indication of a child having such knowledge, would bring not only horrified glances accompanied by outraged scowls from the adults, but a long and disgusted silence would ensue, soon followed by comments such as 'force ripe', 'eggs up', and "big before time" comments directed malevolently towards the hapless child. And all children had experienced and cringed forever with the memory of the sweltering silence and banishment that had befallen them when they had swam into these shark-infested waters.

So it was to prevent myself from being caught in such a web that I had begun to wander from the scene as the strangeness of the adult conversation became too mystifying for my limited powers of absorption and deductions. And it was while I lulled myself into this state of invisibility that I heard the arresting sound. Like the steady hum of distant traffic, it came from just beyond the edge of the green lawn which swept downhill and away from the church. I walked towards the source and then I saw it. The long wide river which I seem to instinctively know is rolling towards the sea in Ocho Rios. I stare into its depths and feel as if I'm looking for something. For someone.

I know this river and I know that something eventful happened here! From the bank where I stand I can see the huge smooth boulders, their white backs like half-submerged creatures rising just above the surface of the swiftly flowing glass-like water. They lie like sleeping creatures as the river churns and rushes over and around them, just as it must have done all those years ago. The women on the other side wave at me - and suddenly, I remember!

Yes! It was a Saturday. I was three or four years old, and I was standing on this very spot with my mother and the pastor. The people on the opposite river bank - whom the pastor had stared at severely as he murmured 'Worldlians', had laughed and frolicked; just as they were doing now. All around them their children swam, while others plunged, dived and played river games like tugging legs under water and squirting mouthfuls of the stuff through their teeth, as squeals of excitement rang out and contrasted with the reverential silence on our side. I watched with longing as the little Worldlians raced each other up and down the sparkling river, plunging their thin dark arms under and over the shining water, battling against the currents.

And now, as then, I hear the occasional call from the women, their mothers and grandmothers, aunts or cousins

'Stapp dat!'

'Behave yuself.'

'Don't let me beat you.'

'A say...' then a pause quickly followed by a decisive warning-like kissing of teeth, 'Let im go! Stap playing so rough!'

Some names are uttered in warning tones

'Silbert!'

'Uroy!'

'Mannish!'

'Dennington! A waaning yu!' Always boys.

The smaller children, mainly girls, sit topless and even naked beside their mothers, playing with dolls or simply whimpering amidst the laughter, while the women from time to time whirl pieces of wet clothes above their heads in a figure of eight motion before they slap them on the rocks and pummel them on the smooth flat stones with vigorous kneading actions. Just as they had done when I had been Girl of the Day, age three, in Sabbath school. For my special day I was wearing the unchanging fashion of a frothy white dress, the streamers flamboyantly tied around the waist and culminating in a big fat bow at my back. To complete the picture of elegance, I wore a white saucer shaped straw hat decorated with bunches of coloured flowers, their stems tucked into the crown under a broad strip of pink grosgrain ribbon, the long ends of which continued down the back of my dress where they made their acquaintance with the waiting bow.

The honour of being Girl of the Day, had involved me being hoisted up without warning onto a table where I was left to dangle my legs freely as all the children sat below on the floor and busied themselves with admiring my shiny shoes and frilly socks from England. I in turn, from my elevated position looked around me at some old things, with fresh eyes.

One familiar object was a picture - a copy of which I

discovered over the years, hung in every house, shop, school, post office, doctor's surgery and hospital I had ever visited. It was large and was of a tall white man with a silky close-cut beard which matched his long straight, whitecoloured shoulder length hair. The lady-like hairstyle rested on his long clean blindingly white robes, from under which peeped toes which jutted out like little pale hardough breads, from his brown strappy sandals. My eyes travelled back upwards to his face which in former times had always been too far above my head, and I noted the redness of his lips and his kind blue eyes which, to my surprise, were fringed in white coloured lashes. Resting in the crook of one arm was a white lamb and in the other hand he held a long stick with a curve at the end. But the thing which now grabbed my attention, was the big red heart which was not inside his chest but instead stood on his white robe and seemed to be wrapped in prickly kuritch thorns. I stared long and hard at the man and the lamb, but mainly at his big red heart. And each time I looked into his piercing blue eyes he seemed to be staring back at me. I stared back curiously and wondered why he wasn't crying.

The teacher smiled at the picture and said that the man's name was Jesus. And while I wondered if we should know him, she read for us the writing below the picture, "Jesus the Lamb of God". She then told us that he was a fisherman who went around with other men that were called Fishers of Men. Following this, we all pretended to row a boat as we sang:

    I will make you Fishers of Men

        Fishers of men

        Fishers of men

I will make you Fishers of Men

If you faal looow me...

In louder voices, we repeated the last line of the song several times and at different decibels, while I tried to remember if I had ever seen anyone looking like the man in the picture, fishing with some other men by the bay in Ocho Rios. Then without any warning, the singing and clapping ended, and I was swung down from the table and placed unceremoniously onto unsteady feet. My time as Girl of the Day had come to an abrupt end.

Now in my mind's eye I can still see the little girl standing on the green lawn which curved along the edge of the glittering silver river that in some parts ran serenely like liquid glass over the glistening boulders. And I can hear my mother laughing and talking with the vicar above my head before they were interrupted by a sudden splash which was followed by an equally sudden silence as the eyes of the congregation travelled down the river to the source of the sound. Down to where something was moving rapidly, rising above and then sinking beneath the churning water; and travelling frantically towards us in a lather of foam. On and on it came, rising and plunging, rising and plunging, closer and closer and closer. The people's voices rose in urgent tones.

'A wa dat?' someone asked as they craned their neck dangerously over the bank to identify the object.

'Ee Eeeee!' another member of the congregation said indignantly.

Quite quickly the 'thing' was identified as a man, and someone asked in a perplexed tone followed by a longkissing of teeth, (which sounded like eggs being plopped into very hot oil) accompanied by a heavy volume of disgust, 'A weh him a do down deer dis time a mawning?'

And in response someone with more than a hint of anger, Bible held securely to their chest answered, 'Me no know!' And after a short pause added, 'Especially as him mus know say de service aawn now.'

Everyone, even the barking dog, now ceased in their activities and watched the rise and fall of the man as he came nearer and nearer using a combination of swimming and wading followed by rising and falling. His shiny black body, like wet coal, rose and desperately plunged beneath the foaming waters while he thrashed his arms up and down in a circular motion. Time and time again, the top of his body erupted from the foaming water which rushed against him as it travelled to the waiting sea. Suddenly there was darkness as my mother's splayed fingers fell across my eyes, just as ripples of laughter from both sides of the river broke the silence. Then blindfold off, I could see that the man was coming closer and closer to us and as the water fell from his shoulders I almost saw all of his body as he shot up from what appeared to be a deep pool. Gasps of horror and disgust came from the congregation, mixed in with a sprinkle of laughter from The Worldlians on the opposite bank. And once more my mother's fingers found themselves across my eyes as the vicar gasped in a strangled awe-filled voice, 'Jesus Christ!'

Jesus Christ? I struggled to be free of my mother's hand, and through the chinks of her fingers I stared in wonder at the man's smooth black face down which ran clear ribbons of water out of his long thickly twisted dreadlocked hair. I stare open-mouthed in awe as he journeyed against the flow of the river using a mixture of walks and lunges to make his escape from the calls, jeers and laughter. Finally free, I looked up at my mother for some answers but she failed to see me as the vicar's fingers now shielded her eyes.

The man, Jesus, was now in the distance and still desperately struggling from boulder to boulder with wild desperate clawing fingers, and I could see that from time to time he glanced fearfully over his shoulders to look at the congregation as they waved the back of their hands at him in a shooing motion. My lips burned with questions about the black man running wildly up the river. And about the white man with blue eyes. And about the white lamb in the painting hanging on the church wall.

But I was a Jamaican child, and I instinctively knew that questions were only to be asked by 'Big People'. So, I first considered the outrage that would be visited on my head. 'Ma!' Someone would say pursing their lips in a disgusted curl while furrowing their brow. 'Yu hear the pickney a question yu?' and adding 'Force-ripe'.

So I found my own answers to my questions.

Who was the man in the picture on the wall if this was Jesus? I decided that the picture of the man with the white face and the white clothes which reached down to his feet was an unfinished picture. I decided while I stood and looked at the gentle river that gave no indication that Jesus had just swam by, that the picture on the wall, and all the other pictures in every house, school and church that I had ever seen were all waiting to be painted black. I had found my answer and I was satisfied.

I re-joined my grandmother and we said our good byes to Miss G.

'Grandma?' I said tentatively.

'Yes dear?' She asked cheerily

Then came my question. 'You know Jesus?'

'Yes dear I do' she said before adding 'He's our Saviour Lord Jesus Christ.'

'Well...did I ever tell you I saw Jesus once... at this church when I was about three or four-years-old ?' I said cautiously while smiling up at her.

She stopped abruptly, and looked down at me as if we had just met.

'What have I told you about telling lies?' she barked before adding the most frightening words any Jamaican child can hear, 'Don't let me have to beat yu!'

Now in self-preservation mode, I hung back a few steps behind her but was determined to play my final card 'I saw him in the river, grandma'. I paused. 'And he was black'.

But the look of horror on her face as she turns to look at me, stops me in my tracks and shrivels my tongue.

The End

It is October 1962. And under the rising heat of the morning sun, the multi-coloured children in their orderly columns, resemble a finely graduated colour wheel which attest not only to the history of the country but to its optimistically apt motto 'Out Of Many One People'.

Ranging in age from seven to fourteen, with a handful bordering on fifteen to maybe twenty years of age, the pupils of Flaxman All Age School, are not only arranged by class. Outside of school, and occasionally during school hours, some are unconsciously judged by an unwritten code, which is left unsaid but felt by many, and which often placed them in a pyramid-like structure with the pale freckle-strewn yellow hues at the top, the highly polished burnished brown gold below, but above an array of almost translucent glowing black foundation. All beautiful, and all innocent, they wait patiently under the dazzlingly blue Caribbean sky for their daily assembly to begin.

Biddable, yet proud, they represent the undisputed truth of their recently revealed motto of Independence from British rule. They stand still, in regulated columns and wait - their shiny upturned faces polished with the sun and daily doses of coconut oil, vaseline and various other emollients. The youngest students stand in the front rows, graduating down to the older and taller ones; with the sixteen to twenty year old boys standing at the very back. All, except for the older boys are separated by an empty space wide enough for a head boy or someone larger to comfortably walk or even to dash down it, depending on whether the task is to distribute pamphlets or to hurriedly remove a disrupter.

Today, like on any other day, they display their sartorial

splendour. Precise as always in every detail down to the last pleat or crease, a testament to the determination of their families to confirm to themselves and to the world that pride is not the preserve of the wealthy. The girls are dressed in crisp white short sleeved cotton blouses under dark blue crisp pinafores, all set with razor-sharp pleats up to the waist and held in place with toning belts. The boys, kept in cohesive columns by the ever-vigilant head boy Alphonso, are for another hour at least, resplendent in light brown freshly laundered khaki, finished with knife sharp creases. Small boys dressed in cream-coloured khaki shorts, display well-oiled knees, while the older boys gratefully hide the evidence of their raging hormones in matching full-length trousers.

But where swift growth spurts coincided with financial privations, many of these garments quickly became what others jokingly termed 'ankle swingers' - often a misnomer as after only a few months of wear, the cuffs of some trousers had long parted company with the wearer's ankles. But a small detail such as trouser length was not allowed by eager parents, to stand in the way of 'gettin a good edication'. And school-refusers, whether absent for reasons of outgrown clothes or for less trivial reasons, were religiously sought out by the community and brought to their place of learning in the strong belief of the righteous apprehender that they were assisting the head teacher in his bid to secure an educated workforce for 'de future of Jumaica'. To that common end, many a violently struggling truant - serial refusers - were returned to school by friends, neighbours, the police, church brethren, or even retired teachers, in their belief that they were participating in the fight against 'rampant illiteracy'; a phrase someone said, conjured up for him an image of a dunce on a wayward horse.

The head boy, Alphonso, tall, sporting a neat haircut and dressed in stone coloured khaki shirt and full-length pants, surveys the serried ranks of his temporary charges.

Someone out of line in one of the poker-straight arrangement is asked 'Which group you in? This one or this one?' while his long straight fingers waves to and fro like a shark's fin.

'Dis one' states the undecided one.

'Well stay there then!' he commands, his words delivered in crisp English pronunciation - a feature that marked him out for the post, and no doubt for future posts of authority beyond his school days. Further along the ranks he displays a forced humour in his voice as he asks a bigger boy in the back row, 'Are you a girl today?' The answer is a curt and questioning 'No?'

To which the response is 'So why are you in the girl's group then? I thought you changed into a girl.'

The subdued chuckling which ensues is swiftly quelled with a firm command to the recalcitrant one, 'Go back to your line!'

Murmurs of discontent arise from those closest to the temporary girl which in turn forces Alphonso to show the source of his authority.

'If I have any backchat from you I can give your name to the head teacher if you want' he threatens, and dissent is instantly quelled before he retires and stands in his position; one step down from where the head teacher stands each day facing his charges until all the classes are dismissed at the end of each assembly. And on cue, Mr. Wilson makes his entrance with all the dash and panache of a Shakespearean actor, ready to perform his lines.

His attire is of a standard required of his station; one which also meets the expectation of the neighbourhood, members of whom can often be heard to remark in satisfied tones to others and to their children, 'Dressed as if for a meeting wid Queen Elizabeth', or 'Im sharp as razor blade in a dat suit.' Today, as usual, he stands on the topmost step in another of his colonial-style suits, white shirt, and with the addition of what some would say is a superfluous addition in view of the blazing sun – a tie.

Each morning that he had stood facing the town, its activities had not interrupted him as he had spoken to his attentive students. Employing a well modulated voice, his words had had a background tapestry of distant shouts, raucous and spontaneous greetings between friends, and even on a few occasions, angry orders given by bosses to workers on roadside projects. There had even been on occasions, the slam of dominoes spilling out through the open windows of the local bar, but never had the attention of his audience with their backs to the town, wavered or strayed from the revered face of their head teacher as he continued his duty of 'Character Building'.

Every passing adult knew that what they observed each day as they went to and fro in their daily endeavours, was not just two columns of their children standing in the morning sun, looking up in adoration and with respect at the man at the top of a short flight of stairs; they knew that they were watching Nation-building. That they were observing a moulding of minds. A forming of character. Yes, they knew with pride that he was there, in front of their very eyes, building a better Jamaica. And it was a job for which he had been given full authority to conduct; not only by the education officers from Kingston but also from the general population, many of whom had been taught by the self-same man when he was little more than a boy. He the head teacher, Mr. H. Wilson, in their eyes, was beyond reproach; the one person who they knew single-handedly on a daily basis, fought battles against illiteracy. And won.

And to aid him in that fight, the whole village felt a responsibility, and so contributed in any small way they could. So apart from the various physical gifts given in every form to this saviour of the nation - from a haircut to first produce of the yearly harvest, to first eggs from a new clutch of hens - they aimed for an even loftier gift during his assemblies. The general population's main endeavour was to travel noiselessly about their daily business beyond the picket fence which surrounded the school grounds. So, loud music, loud arguing would cease and even braying overloaded buses would creep wheezing by on struggling engines. And on one occasion the unoiled creaking of a bicycle was suddenly quelled after a stern stare from Mr Wilson; or maybe it was just the onset of extreme fatigue of the rider which caused it to cease in its creaking. It was later discovered by the children, that the said bicycle had been carried uphill on the shoulders of its respectful owner.

Sometimes if the children looked closely at the face of the head teacher they could deduce the never-ending story of the Content Road according to the subtle changes in his many expressions. A silent waved greeting would elicit a fleeting smile and a hardly perceptible nod of the head while the spotting of a truanting student would result in the sudden narrowing of his eyes which they the children knew, held a promise of retribution for the school-refuser. The occasional unkindness inflicted on one passer-by to another would register with an unflinching stare, and a shifting of his feet suggested that someone was not adhering to his unwritten but widely acknowledged rule of silence.

It was in October, two months after Jamaican Independence from British rule, during one of these nation-building assemblies, that the ever-attentive children had watched with rising alarm the outraged expression on the head teacher's face as the car had come to a screeching stop behind them. Keen ears had surmised the make of the vehicle and they had instinctively known it to be of the sports variety. Children and adults alike were enamoured with American manufactured cars, and they were inspected at every opportunity; their sleekness and leather interiors noted, their sounds on being revved up committed to memory, before each specimen was finally placed in a pecking order of beauty. And the sports car was always at the top of the list. So now, they had all silently and emphatically conveyed to each other, with a satisfied smirk, that yes, it had to be, indisputably, a sports car. A red one!

Like statues they stood, facing forward, and ached to be granted, just this once, the chance to turn around and see this beauty.

But the unwritten rule prevented this luxury, as they knew that to turn around and present their backs to their head teacher was, an unthinkable act. So with ears pricked, they listened keenly to the sweet purring of the engine of this automobile which had fun and games written into its name.

With the rule uppermost in their minds, they had with unseeing eyes, stared intently at the head teacher, who steadfastly persisted in sharing a passage from his large and well-thumbed Bible. His lips moved but his words fell on deaf ears, and above his head writ large on the banner which had miraculously materialised and now blazed like the sun into their staring eyes, were the words which said plainly and authoritatively, 'NO TURNING WHILE THE HEADTEACHER IS STANDING ON THE STEPS IN FRONT OF YOU! And they knew that any deviation from the rule would result in very serious consequences of an unknown kind. It would surely, they decided, be as bad as what befell Lot's wife. And there would be nothing worse, the younger more impressionable children thought, than being turned into a pillar of salt. So while every fibre of their bodies strained and fought against the instinctive need to use their rigid eyes to see what lay behind them, they valiantly struggled to fix their feet firmly forward on the ground; to many, an effort equal to not swallowing a piece of delicious cake. Instead, while the head teacher droned on and the car stood behind their rigid backs, they thought of what the consequences of failure might be.

Dissension they knew would certainly earn them a visit to the head's study and an unwelcome encounter with the cane. The dreaded cane with which a proportion of the older ones had had a previous encounter, and which they knew, when it was not in service, hung lazily, innocuously, and bored, on a hook just inside the head teacher's office. But even worse was the knowledge that offenders might first be caned, then ordered to leave the school forever; and then forever and a day, amen, be pointed at in the street as a failure. Known as someone who had cut short the promise of an education which, who knows, could have brought financial security and a fulfilment of dreams which had been deferred for centuries. So with their heads, as one, swimming with visions of calamities that could befall them, they stood and tried desperately to tune their ears to the words which came in a mumble of sounds from the headmaster's taut lips.

But his pearls of wisdom wafted away on the wind as the taunts of the ever purring engine roared inside their heads and made them burn with a desire to look, to admire what lay behind their rigid backs. Oh, how they needed to know the colour of the car, and to see who was lucky enough to drive it. They pondered, was it Mr Walker the rich grandfather one of their classmates who stood amongst them and who also bore a face rigid with inquisitiveness? Or was it one of the Bower's boys recently arrived with new riches from America to which the family sallied back and forth on almost a weekly basis. Or the twin sons of the Cossen's family who lived abroad somewhere and regularly flaunted their spoils on the admiring locals. Or could it be one of the Deputy Head's son who had left Jamaica after a disagreement and had now returned, having made his way in the world. Or maybe it was Lainey's father who worked in the cane fields of Cuba and who always came back home with a new gold watch which when strategically displayed, always caught the rays of the sun and glittered for the benefit of admiring onlookers.

Then a sound splintered their thoughts. Loud, long and impatient, the horn sent its audacious reverberations all around the school, up and down the Content Road and into their rigid bodies. All other sounds ceased before another one quickly followed the first. Longer and louder. A tsunami-like surge of emotions ran amongst the startled children and they stiffened as their eyes bore pleadingly into those of the head teacher and beseeched him to instantly and without any ceremony, abolish the unwritten rule. Just this once. Just so they could stare at the face of the mad man who had disrespected him. But before he could grant them their wish, a treble-blasting of the horn, almost like a dance tune, rang out. And this time it was accompanied by a friendly-sounding greeting of 'Hi kids!' The salutation, when it came, was in a familiar accent. One which sounded as if a mouthful of nuts and shells were being chewed, and it informed the 'kids', as they were deemed, that their visitors were Americans. The very people who daily, walked and talked through their books, their advertisements, brochures, and their lives in an island dependent on tourism.

So, like dutiful children who had been taught to speak when spoken to, they responded in the only way they knew. To always be polite to adults. So now there were no preliminary sidelong glances. No surreptitious peeping through curious fingers while pretending to smooth damp foreheads in a bid to take a sneaky glance. No. They swallowed the cake. Caution was thrown to the wind. And as one, they turned around. Their backs now to their head teacher, finally they were able to also see what they had only heard. Yes, just as they thought, it was a sports car. And yes! It was red, and even more amazing, there was not just one, but two, Americans! Excitement and expectations rose within their curious bodies.

The pair, a man and a woman leaned back nonchalantly on their open-topped car. Both were tall, blond and with big teeth revealed by even bigger smiles. The children stared back at the people who came from the place that filled their daily dreams. The place of big houses, big cars, and of course, the biggest ice-creams! Sighs of satisfaction wafted amongst them as they looked on wide-eyed and with the honest non-judgemental curiosity that only children can display. The younger ones, no longer in the front row, craned their necks like thirsty travellers seeking an oasis, in a bid to satisfy their desire to see the exotic visitors. And the pair stared back confidently at the waiting children with mischievous lopsided grins on their tanned faces, and seemed as though they were preparing for a game; almost as one would stare at a dog before a stick was thrown. The happy smiling children stared back in awe. But some did wonder why these two friendly people had not entered the grounds, met their head teachers and be treated to the usual hospitality reserved for all visitors. The iced drinks, the bowls of fruits, the paper-thin sandwiches made from the national hardough bread with the best bit, the crust, trimmed off. And followed by the sweet bun, laden down with delicious creamy Jamaican cheese, nicely rounded off with steaming mint tea served from the prettiest of teapot, and poured into the tiniest bone china cups. Yes, served in the English way. But the children accepted this new form of visiting, and waited.

Then out of the blue it happened. In the slowest of slow motion. The sudden movement of the man's hand drew their eyes upwards, as still smiling, he threw his clenched fist high into the bright blue sky and they watched, mesmerised, as he flung it right back, back, back behind his blonde head. Back as far as he could until it seemed to pause in space, its shape like a golden hammer, dramatically outlined by the blazing sun. And spellbound, the polite and dutiful children watched in silence as with greater speed and force the young man brought his weapon-like arm to the fore. Forward, forward, forward, with a strength which seemed designed to strike and annihilate an invisible foe. Forward into the foreground it came, with his fist still curiously clenched, he brought it finally to its full extension and they gasped in amazement as his hand flew open and from the centre of his palm, surrounded by his splayed and rigid fingers, all silhouetted against the yellow sun, there came, like a flock of frightened birds, what seemed to be hundreds of spinning and twirling golden objects. The children watched, open mouthed, as an arc of circular shapes spun wildly against the sun and the bright blue sky, before they descended, and one by one landed noiselessly onto the green lawn which lay between them. With their hands now shielding their eyes, the smaller children, positioned behind the taller and stockier ones, peeped and craned their necks through nooks and crannies, and tried to decipher what the golden creatures were that had emerged from the strong magical fist of their new friend. They waited expectantly to see the jumps and leaps of some new American creatures.

But something even more dramatic happened. From the front of the crowd, came a boy's hoarse and jubilant cry. In a voice like a sudden clap of thunder, he bellowed

"Money!" There was a roaring repetition of the word.

"Money!" "Money!" "Money!" And their tone suggested a culmination of all their hopes and dreams. A longing, a desperation, and a prayer answered. The roar of the magic word rose to a crescendo, then something like a charge of electricity ignited the crowd and in slow motion, the big boys with arms no longer at their sides and no longer standing in regimental rows, but with sharp rigid elbows and muscular legs prepared and straining like determined sprinters, they moved towards the bounty. They charged in one huge boiling mass. Leaping, whooping and guffawing as they sprang upon the unexpected treasure. And as each piece of the quarry was spied as though with an eagle's eye trained upon its prey, they leapt, struggled, bellowed, and fought for their unexpected treasure. They clawed at the lawn and fell in scattered struggling heaps, rolling on top of each other, tearing at each other under the billowing Jamaican flag. They screamed, shoved, pushed and grappled, tearing epaulettes from shoulders, buttons from shirts, and pockets from newly pressed trousers. All in their bid to gather the unexpected windfall.

But the once smiling couple no longer smiled. Now they laughed with glee as their cameras whirred and clicked and flashed as they recorded all the actions of the gladiatorial scenes of greed, hunger and anger. A boy scooped up some money. Click! A boy elbowed another boy out of the way. Click! Click! A boy jumped on another boy to get his money back. Click! Click! Click! Two boys had a fist fight over a perceived wrong. Click! Click! Click! Blood ran down the face of one boy, Click! Then the spectacle ended as suddenly as it had begun. Without a wave of goodbye or a flashing smile, the pair with mocking grins, jumped into their purring sports car and sped away along the busy Content Road, the triumphant roar of their revving engine blowing in the wind on its journey to the Ocho Rios tourist resort.

Now the children, enveloped in shame, stood shamefaced and bereft while the bounty hunters with heads hung low, dragged themselves with heavy steps back to their designated places. Silence hung expectantly in the air, and slowly, one by one each pupil looked up from under hooded eyes, into the face of the man they most respected and feared. Seeking forgiveness, they looked, with desperation in their eyes, into a face now etched with sadness and disappointment. And in an alien and distant voice which bore the tremors of fatigue, their head teacher stood tall and regal as he delivered in a staccato style, a set of instructions, in short and unemotional bursts. He said as if reading from a book, 'Beware of false smiles.'

Then a pause while his eyes raked the back rows where the big boys stood. 'Don't let people fool you with money.'

He silently gathered his papers before he once more surveyed the sea of guilty faces. Then in a voice laden with warning he continued 'And don't allow anyone to ever make you feel that they're more important than you'

Another pause. The children waited to hear what their punishment would be. He continued 'Regardless of the colour of their skin'.

Then picking up his notes and Bible he turned his back on his audience, for the first time ever, and was gone. Bereft with shame, their eyes followed his exit and everyone knew that tomorrow, even if the Angel Gabriel was to fly down from the bright blue cloudless sky and blow his trumpet into every individual ear, they would not - unless directed by the head teacher - turn their backs on him, ever again.

For today they had learnt the meaning of respect and self-respect.

The End

Man Shearing Ice

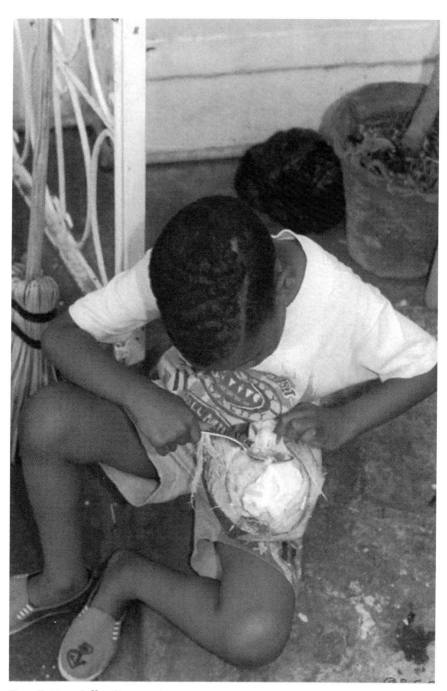

Boy Eating Jelly Coconut

Man Husking Coconuts

Man Making Ice-Cream

Puppies are coming

I had been forbidden to read the newspapers because I was only eight years old and the nature of the news found between the pages was thought to be unsuitable for my constitution. Once, I'd heard my grandma, with a chuckle, murmur to my grandad after I had been innocently trying to decipher some writing on her bottle of medicine, 'Why they (the school, I supposed) couldn't have teach her to read when she was a bit older? She too inquisitive sometimes.'

And following my grandad's conspiratorial smile at me, she had added, 'In my day, children couldn't read til dey was well pass nine years old.'

At this point I had quickly adopted a well-practised still and invisible stance, and satisfied, they had enjoyed their joke with a silent shoulder-shaking chuckle.

After sleep had overtaken them, I read greedily and with speed, of the gory details of events taking place in 'foreign' before my eyes had against my will, travelled to the very bottom of the paper. This was a space usually reserved for things my grandma raged against as being silent killers of people - cigarettes and alcohol. This space was usually the permanent home of bottles of honey coloured drinks accompanied by glasses poised at a festive angle and heaped full of refreshing ice held by hands adorned with twinkly bracelets and chunky flashing wrist watches. In some editions of the paper the yellow drinks were replaced by tantalising packets of cigarettes, the bottoms of which seemed to have been knocked on a hard surface which always dislodged just one of the killer sticks out of the pack; the previous one was always being smoked by a man who always leaned against a tree staring into the horizon and bearing an expression of contentment on his face, while curls of whitish grey smoke seemed to escaped gently from his slightly pursed lips and towards his half closed eyes. But today, those murderers (my grandmother's words again) were on holiday and had been replaced by the big black letters which were at least an inch high and almost as wide. They said loudly, **PUPPIES ARE COMING...** and they stretched across two whole pages, in a lay-waiting style. Poised and ready to spring out at the unsuspecting reader just as they prepared to turn the page. I was gripped by their confidence. By their assertiveness. Their certainty. And the three dots which accompanied the words promised so much that I almost expected the puppies to leap out as I slowly turned the page. I peeped overleaf, but to my surprise, there were no puppies. Just more news about people behaving badly in foreign parts. And the cigarettes and brown drinks were there too.

But the words had worked their magic. I was gripped. Hush puppies? I was intrigued. What sort of puppies were they? I wondered. Prising my eyes away from the paper I looked beyond the confines of the veranda and at our own dogs strolling lazily about, and tried to imagine how different these Hush Puppies would be from our lovely dogs. Would they remain puppies all their lives? And why were they called 'Hush'? What was special about them?

Did they have special feet to walk softly past Mr Bennet's shop? They would have to be careful of the road because all the big trucks from Kingston stopped at his shop, delivering buns and bread, tinned milk and cereals, millions of bottles of beer, and tons of sweets. And where I wondered, were they coming from?

My mind roved across the parts of Jamaica that I knew.

If they were coming from Kingston they would have a very long journey. They would have to be careful of the road because being on a main road, lots of cars would be travelling down too. Or maybe they were coming from Ocho Rios where lots of tourists arrived from different countries. Maybe they were bringing the puppies to Jamaica.

And where I wondered, were these puppies going? A wave of excitement suddenly engulfed me as the thought crossed my mind that maybe they were coming here to Pleasant farm. Maybe my grandad had ordered some more dogs. I glanced across at my two dozing grandparents and made a mental note to ask them about these puppies.

In the meantime, I considered how the puppies with the special silent features would travel all the way from Ocho Rios where my brother Ludlow lived. I imagined that if they were travelling by foot they would have to make sure they kept to the sidewalk which ran along the seafront and restaurants, past the gift shops, and up to Tower Isles where the best hotels and uncle Buttley's tailor shop were. From there they would travel some way before they reached Content where they would go past my favourite shop which sold not only the prettiest and best dresses, bags and hats in the most wonderful designs and colours, but also a wide variety of fabrics and American paper patterns. They would then travel past the welder's shop opposite the little post office which stood well back from the road in a pretty little garden with its meandering crazypaving path. From there they would walk past Mr Willis' tailor shop and Mr Cecil's carpenter shop which was next door to Mr. Aubrey's car and bicycle mechanic shop where there always seemed to be a party going on with just a few people but a lot of noise. Next, they would have to travel up to the big market where the butchers and also the kind green grocers had their shops. Then past the baker whose shop always had mounds of Jamaican cakes, bullas, bread and a whole variety of pastries where large groups of children would linger every day after school, just sniffing the air if they didn't have any money to buy anything. If by then the puppies hadn't been picked up and taken home by other people they would have to walk past the Flaxhill All Age School and then past the row of Chinese grocery shops that stood half a mile further along the Content Road; one of these shops many people said, sold the best sweets and ice-creams found anywhere in Jamaica. When Miss Vie our helper had heard these comparisons, she had chuckled privately and said that as some of these people had never travelled out of the district she didn't know what they were comparing the taste to.

The journey of the puppies would continue for about two more miles, past lots of big houses half hidden behind hedges and gardens until they came to Retreat church, next to the police station which stood on a gentle sloping hill on the right. If they were thirsty they could drink some water from the river which was across the road from the police station and the church which ran, on its way to the sea in Ocho Rios, under the scary swinging bridge. After drinking they could continue on the Retreat Road and past the dark wooded place where, in my vivid imaginings, the story of Lorna Doone took place. Finally, they would travel along the outer wall of the hidden cemetery and turn left at the big Poinsietta tree where they would walk for a little while before turning left into Pleasant Farm. They could then crawl under the big iron gate which "separates and protects us", according to my grandad, from potential robbers. From there they could travel up the L shaped drive to our house, where me and Miss Vie our helper would give them some food and water, or even some cool milk from the fridge. I wondered, in my daydream, if they also liked ripe bananas, because even though my grandad exported a lot to England, we also kept a lot for ourselves.

Curiosity, or "Fass" was what my grandma said was the proper word, gripped me. Infected by waves of excitement I was overcome by a heady feeling of dizziness. The pit of my stomach was on fire. I needed answers. But to ask would have revealed that I had not followed my grandparent's instructions about not reading the newspapers. I tried to find some hidden clues to the mystery by reading and rereading the surprising announcement. Questions to which I tried to find my own answers marshalled themselves into my consciousness. What sort of dogs were Hush Puppies? Where were they coming from? What would they look like? I hoped they'd be small, soft and fat. Would they be friendly? I also wanted to know if they'd be big like our dogs who according to the sign at the start of our drive, were dangerous and should be 'Be-wared' of; or would they be friendly like 'Tear Up' who was our too-gentle yard dog. My imagination continued to do somersaults and back flips. With my possible providers of answers fast asleep and audibly snoring, I relied on my own deductions and formulated some further pictures in my mind.

I could see them. They were huge brown silky creatures with round gentle eyes, floppy ears, and soft padded soundless feet. One yawned and I spied its huge lolling velvet tongue that I imagined would silently lick someone to death if they stroked them. I could see them bowling me over as we played, and then not knowing their own strength I sensed that they would trample over playmates and leave them flattened in a star shape as people were often portrayed in my Sunday comics. Then their huge furry tails would swish, swish, swish across my face as I tried to find my feet. Or maybe, I mused, they were called Hush Puppies because they were silent. Because they didn't have a bark! If so, then maybe they would be good for creeping up on burglars. Maybe, I thought, they should be called 'Burglar Dogs', not 'Hush Puppies'. I wanted to see one and so I decided that whatever the penalties for reading the grownup newspapers, I would quiz my grandparents about these puppies.

I returned the papers to their original state of disarray and searched the snoozing face of my grandmother for hints of wakefulness. Slowly, after emitting a few dry coughs she came wide awake to find my face with two desperate eyes boring into her. Alarm and fear were equally shared by us both and resulted in a shout from her of 'Why yu keep a look so hard in a mi face when a trying to sleep pickney?' This was followed by a dissatisfied 'Cho' which summed up the fact that this situation had occurred previously and was the reason for many of her naps being cut short. Shaken but not deterred, I began tentatively

'Granma suppose someone brought some new dogs here'.

'What sart of dawgs' she said suspiciously

'Some dogs that didn't have a bark'

It could have been my imagination but I thought I caught a

hint of unexploded laughter in her voice before she replied in a somewhat high pitched tone.

'I neva hear of dawgs without barks, dear' she said throwing a mysterious glance at my now wide-awake grandad.

'Well,' I continued, convinced that they were not aware of the source of my knowledge 'Suppose they were a special type of dogs?'

'Den,' said my grandma suppressing what now definitely sounded like a stifled chuckle, 'We'd have to call them hush puppies', and she quickly looked at my grandad whose eyes also appeared to be shining as though he was on the verge of tears.

He stared back at her in silence, then finally asked me

'Where yu hear about dese dawgs Cassandra?'

'Nowhere grandad. I was just wondering if some of them would come here.'

'Don't you worry yuself about any strange dawgs coming here Cassie. Dese Jamaican dawgs wouldn't tolerate any new dawgs coming and laading it ova dem.'

'But if they're nice dogs, they could come here?' I asked hopefully.

And with the confidence of the successful owner of a big taxi rank at Tower Isles hotel he added, 'Nothing is coming to dis country. And if it come here, I will know about it.' Then with a hint of pride he added, 'Nothing at all can come into dis country widout me hearing about it'. But in spite of their confident reassurances, I thought about this new breed of dog for the whole week and I couldn't wait for Sunday to come again, to discover more.

The days crawled by slowly. Monday. Too slow.

Tuesday. Go away. Wednesday. Neither here nor there.

Thursday. Make way, make way for Friday. At last.

Saturday. Crawling like a snail. Sunday! Hooray! But first, church had to be borne. Then home! The commentary and the fresh pages of the bulky Sunday papers tossed about over my head while I trawled through the supplementary comic with its gamut of cartoon characters engaging in dubiously hilarious antics which held no interest for me today. The behaviour of Mutt and Jeff, or tall and short as they were sometimes referred to, were usually so hilarious but now passed over my head and left me bored. And as for Minnie the Minx, with her Afro hairstyle and who according to my grandma must have been modelled on me, held no interest for me at all. I did not want drawings of people getting up to useless pranks. I wanted real news. I wanted to know about those puppies.

So, subterfuges were employed to peep into the pages of their big papers. First, I slid onto my gran's commodious lap, but she kissed her teeth softly, shook the paper, and gently budged me out of place by crossing her legs. Next, I tried sidling up to my granddad to look into his portion of the paper but surprisingly it had stuff I knew nothing about. Things called Stocks, and some called Shares. And there were some pictures of farms and cattle; none of which at that moment held any interest for me.

Time ticked on as they pored over the never-ending columns of tiny writing. Precious time during which they exchanged little bits of information from their own portion of newspaper, and little pauses during which they shared jokes and had their usual chuckles over comments that did not seem in the least bit funny.

Finally, the moment arrived! Performing a wide yawn which showed her tonsils, my gran discarded her paper and I watched with great interest as it careered heavily with a dull thud onto the polished red tiles of the veranda floor. But my feelings of elation were dashed as my grandad said,

'A don't know what the world coming to wid all dis fighting and killing all ova the place.'

My grandma displayed her agreement by making a sound with her teeth which sounded like a small fish landing in very hot oil, before she added, 'So long as dey don't start fighting and killing in England. I worry about Elisa and Alston, and of course my biggest granddaughter Freyda.' My grandad keen to allay her fears added in a convincing voice

'Dat Queen Elizabeth is a good woman. She won't let anybody come and disturb har country again. Nat afta dey jus finish one war against dat mad man Hitla'

'A hope yu right Sam' She replied 'All we can do is pray for dem. God is our protector.'

And together they looked out across their acres of land as if they hoped to see the Mother country in the distance. Then in the heat of the afternoon, while the birds twittered away in the surrounding trees and the cows gently mooed in the distant pasture, they slowly drifted off and left me, wide awake, and to my own devices.

Free at last! Without rustling a page, I frantically and hungrily searched for the large black letters. Not there. No not there. Then there they were! Now even bigger and seemingly blacker than before. And they ran over two adjacent pages, but they still gave the same disappointing news.

HUSH PUPPIES ARE COMING...

Now disappointment galvanised me into action. I decided that someone at the newspaper offices had left out an important punctuation mark and had put too many fullstops at the end of the sentence. As my grandad had said, there were no special dogs arriving in Jamaica so I decided that just some ordinary puppies were on their way. So using my pen to make the necessary corrections, I adjusted the sentence to look like this:

HUSH! PUPPIES ARE COMING...

There! I had solved the mystery. Only ordinary puppies were coming, but people had to be quiet so as not to frighten them as they were very nervous puppies. The mystery had been solved. I was quite happy now. But I still wanted to see the puppies. I waited in quivering anticipation for another week to pass.

Sunday arrived, and once again church had to be endured. But on the vicar's final word which signalled our release, I silently but politely pushed my way through the throngs which included the huge family of Bowers who were seeking an audience, as usual, with the vicar. Past enormous handbags stationed at head height and bulging with bibles, hymn books and secret stashes of food left over from breakfast 'for the long service', and out of the clutches of my friends waiting to play. Free at last! With my long-strapped handbag safely strung across my chest and half hidden in the folds of organza and net of my dress, I leapt at speed down the three steps and headed for home. No, today was not a day for waiting to exchange chit chat and jokes with friends, nor for lingering around groups of adults, hoping to catch snippets of their interesting conversations, nor for engaging in games with others while sauntering home along the Content Road. Today I had business to attend to. I needed to get home urgently for the freshly delivered Sunday papers. The ones in which I would find the solution to the mystery of the puppies. Surely there'd be a picture.

So I hurry past the police station after pausing briefly to respond with a wave to the police officer's call of 'Miss Cass!', then swiftly past my worst nightmare - the swinging bridge across which I could only be lured with the promise of sweets, and past the home of the white Americans who had visited us on a few occasions and at whose house I had discovered the secret garden surrounded by tall well clipped hedges which my very clever well-travelled grandad who knew everything had said was called 'Box', and where in amongst the flower beds stately peacocks strutted elegantly about on a velvety lawn, just like in my reading books. Next, I hurry past the spooky place with large dark overhead trees and which to me was Exmoor in England where Lorna Doone and the bad men lived. Then round the bend in the road where the trees parted company overhead and allowed the sun to shine through and send dappled shades onto the hot asphalt, before my arrival at the quiet dark glade where the big poinsettia tree spread its rigid limbs right across the wide road. The very place where I had seen a throng of boys pretending to have spied a cat in the dark mysterious foliage before turning as one and mocking me with taunts of 'Miss Thomas cat', the nickname bequeathed to me because of my fear of cats. Then at last, a sharp left turn past the dreaded cemetery brought me to the double wings of our iron gates, and home.

But today there was to be no careful opening and closing of those gates. No attempt to protect a frilly church dress or shiny leather T-bar shoes sent from England. No. With one hand clutching my bag while the other gripped the curled ironwork, I climb the barrier and negotiated my downward journey, backwards - hardly pausing to land before I set off briskly along the L shaped drive, past the banana and orange groves, getting closer and closer to the coolness of the veranda, the Sunday papers, and the puppies.

But my grandparents are already reading the coveted papers. Leisurely they perused the noisy pages and made comments which they batted to and fro across my head. Opinions about what the world was coming to, the ungodly things people were doing in America, and the changes that were taking place in a country called Africa. I sipped my cool drink while trying to appear unruffled and waited for sleep to engulf them. Before long, their energies, sapped as usual by reports of disarray in foreign land as well as by the heat, the newspapers flutter gently to the floor.

Keeping a watchful eye on them, I carefully and quietly turned the pages, past stories of bloody wars, terrible deaths and dire destruction. Then there it was! But what a surprise. Instead of the words being along the very bottom of two pages as they had been before, the words were now situated on the right-hand side of the newspaper and were of giant proportions, with each word sitting commandingly in its own space. They stated authoritatively

HUSH
PUPPIES
ARE
HERE

My heart thumped as my gaze travelled down to see a picture of a large floppy eared dog with sad limpid eyes sitting morosely next to a very large pair of puppy-coloured shoes. And inside each shoe there was a label identifying as them HUSH PUPPIES.

My heart sank and my body shook with disappointment as I vowed silently never to read the big papers again.

I studied the face of the dog and decided that he looked just the way I felt. Very sad.

The End

Cluster of Coconuts

Fabulous Fishes

Mature Sugar Cane

Ocho Rios High Street

Bunch of bananas

Strong ropes of Wis

Young sugar cane

Wayside greengrocers

In this story, set in Jamaica in the late 1950's, the narrator recalls in conversation with her grandmother, with whom she had lived as a child, a shocking event which reveals in the telling, many cultural practices and beliefs of the Jamaican people. As the story unfolds over almost two decades, the reader discovers that the little girl's responses to her frightening experiences highlights not only the innocence of children but the universality of childhood understanding and their interpretations of events.

Jamaica, August 1977 and I have returned from England to my childhood home.

Around the mid nineteen fifties, my enterprising father like thousands of other Jamaicans and other West Indian islanders, had responded to the call for help from the Mother Country, eager to rebuild itself after the destruction wreaked by the Second World War. After my mother, and later my sister were sent for to join my father who had gone ahead of them some years before, my younger brother and I were left behind - he in the care of our aunt and her husband, and I with my grandparents on their vast farm in the town of Retreat. So, for the next seven years, until the call came to join our parents in the 'Motherland', I lived a life of comfort, security and to some extent, luxury.

And now, after fourteen long years and an adult, I'm back at Pleasant Farm enjoying a six weeks sojourn in the sun. I'm sitting with my widowed grandmother, surrounded by a cornucopia of flora, fauna and fabulous foodstuffs which range from ripe and golden freckle skinned bananas to boulder sized jelly coconuts with the juices just waiting to be consumed straight from the enormous bowl-like shells. Then there are the lush sugar canes growing like long shiny broomsticks, and just about standing, bent under the weight of their thick syrup within. And the palm-sized glossy oranges, so ripe and juicy that they hang heavy and pendulous on the straining branches of tiny trees; all specially grafted and developed decades before by my grandfather, the hobby botanist. My grandmother, Mrs. O Walker of Pleasant Farm and I are engaged in relaxed conversation about events which span the years since I was sent for to join the exodus to England, and also those years when I had lived with her and her husband, Mass Sam. I look at her and do not see the years that have passed. Her ebony coloured face is still beautiful and her now black and white hair is still styled as before - coiled in two German-like plaits around her head. I smile as I remember her collection of hats and hat-pins.

'Gran do you remember how, as a little girl, I was fascinated with your hat pins? I couldn't understand why you stuck them into your head.'

She throws her head back and laughs. 'Yes dear, A rememba the ansa A always use to give you.' she begins in her informal home-only Jamaican patois, 'To stap ma hat flying off into de road and blowing aanda cars'.

'But I always felt sorry for you granma, cause I really used to think that you were sticking the pins into your head!'

We laugh in unison with the memory and she continues 'Or sometimes A use to say, To stap it blowing aff fa daawgs to chase it'.

We muse over the image she has conjured up and our laughter disturbs and alerts the one remaining guard dog dozing and dreaming a few feet away. He raises his massive head to scan the L shaped drive then returns to his napping.

So here we sit side by side, my gran and I; my surrogate mother for seven long years, in a similar way to how we must have done many years ago - but then with me on a smaller chair - and we talk about the years which have separated us since aged eleven when I had become a part of the emigrating throngs that formed the unfounded nightmare of Mr. Enoch Powell's 'Rivers of Blood' speech.

We recall events that have happened at the farm over the past sixteen years, such as the death of Mass Sam as he was referred to by almost everyone including his workers and family members, and about my cousin Ernest who had gone to live in Kingston to work in the rapidly developing television industry. We also talk about how the once productive farm, with its host of workers in the fields and others around the house such as the cook, gardener and sometimes an errand boy all had to be laid off when the main breadwinner had died. And indeed, as I looked around I could see the results of the changes. Lawns less lush, gravel drive bereft of new gravel, gnarled unpruned orange trees, less flowers in the beds, and less dogs and chickens sauntering about.

However, not one for pitying herself, my grandmother quickly assured me that she is well provided for. That as well as having a weekly cleaner, 'Still Miss Vie' for whom she tidies up in advance, the villagers come from time to time to say hello and ask for some of the produce from her land.

'I always let dem help dem self. A just tell dem to have what they need so lang as they pick some for me while they're getting theirs'. She is laughing as she continues 'A caan take it with me Cass'.

She assures me that she lives a contented and comfortable life. She also points to the garage from where the fins of the blue American car peep out. That, she says, will never be driven by her but she can call on a driver if she needs to get somewhere in a hurry or needs to get some shopping. She also 'of course' has the help of almost all of her ten children and numerous grandchildren, some of whom, she says glancing at me, *'Come and stay in your old room from time to time'.*

I reminisce with her about the joys of the warm unhurried days I had spent with her and my grandad. The freedom to roam for hours around the acres of land while surveying and sampling the produce of the fruit trees, observing and smelling the wide variety of flowers and basking in the rays of the yellow sun.

When I paused in my reverie I tell her of the delight I experienced every day when I had fed the numerous chickens with their food which had sat in the huge bowl overnight. As I speak I could almost feel the warmth of the chopped coconut and sweetcorn as each morning I had plunged my fingers deep into the mixture and with palms full and overflowing and using every bit of strength, I had hurled the food as far as I could onto the lawn amongst the hordes of expectant chickens, and watched as they greedily pushed and shoved each other to get at the tasty morsels. At the sight and I expect, smell of the food, the late arrivals had come careering from all corners of the farm with long, drunken and unsteady strides. Some of these, with desperation written all over their faces, had ran, half-flown and stumbled like elderly people who had recently thrown away their very necessary crutches. Jumping and jostling, they had all charged forward clucking, and had eaten until their stuffed craws were very visible under their glossy multi-coloured feathers. My granma laughs and reminds me of how after Errol had come to live with us, I had fought for the right to retain my chicken-feeding duties.

Deep in reflection about my idyllic childhood, I am about to plunge a mouthful of teeth into my umpteenth mango, when I sense that my granma is staring at me. She leans forward and looks into my face as she asks the question which transforms my own face into a grimace. I freeze.

Teeth bared, and mango poised. I look back deep into her eyes and repeat her question. "Do I remember the man?" Her question is so unexpected and reminds me of something so shocking that my eyes, while I speak, continue to stare unblinkingly at her. Then my memory, like an old film on an ancient projector, jumps, whirs and reverses through time. Then judders to a halt. It is 1960. As my breathing accelerates, and the loaded film begins to play, I answer in a voice devoid of doubt, 'Yes grandma. I remember him.'

Now I sit and we recall the events of that day. A day which had begun just like any other day.

Yes, I can see him clearly now. 'In fact,' I say, discarding what would have been my fourth delicious mango, 'I have never forgotten him.'

'You really do?' she asks, surprised.

'Yes grandma.' I pause. 'As clearly as if it had happened yesterday. I was eight' I said.

She said 'Yes, it was the haliday. You were at big school by then.' She chuckled in a mirthless fashion, 'You have a good memory, Cassie.'

The day had begun like any other day...

Morning had arrived in its usual, flamboyant Jamaican fashion, with fierce sunshine forcing its way through my cotton curtains, from what I know as I lay in bed, is definitely a blue, cloudless sky. As usual, the cockerel, clothed in his fluffed-out and magnificently iridescent party wear, is standing, I also know, on his usual post at the corner of the cow pasture as he belts out his raucous but rhythmic cock-a-doodle-doos. Next comes the harsh monosyllabic cawings of the peacocks, who although they sleep in or under the trees at the far side of the farm, are making their way regally towards the open, wide arena of the lawn where at feeding time, they present a show of their lustrous green feathers, each decorated with a large, black, unseeing eye. Then as if to add some new notes to the cacophony of sounds, the repetitive and demanding barking of our dogs can be heard. Their orchestra of sounds range from a rasping yapping of the younger ones to the warning tenor of the larger guard dogs. Then finally, to this animal racket is added the soft baritone lowing of the cows in the far pasture - striving not to be excluded but also determined to remind us humans that they are ready to be relieved of their milk.

I ask my gran who is silently eating one of many mangoes that we've lined up for a feast 'Do you remember that I was usually up long before anyone?'

'Yes, mi dear' she laughs, 'Even after Errol come to live you would race him to get to the pear tree. Cass,' she continues 'Yu rememba how yu use to love to walk around the property as if you own it?' and she looks off into the distance and chuckles at the memory...

'Oh grandma, you don't know how much I loved living here with you both. Every day was like living in a story book. It really was."'

Now in the flowerbeds, I stop to take a close look at my favourite mystery. The dew. I examine the magical globules of water which congregate on each leaf and bud overnight. Look at their half spherical shapes, and the way they lay silently on the leaves and petals like multifaceted glass prisms, slightly shivering and reflecting their surroundings in the tiniest of miniature pictures.

'Remember how the dawgs use to love yu?' Says my gran.

'Yes, I don't know how they knew that I was awake' I reply.

The friskiest of these, Tear-up, had on his arrival at Pleasant Farm been only a tiny little puppy with a very patchy coat and we had named him 'Tearup' based on his appearance and because of the look of his teeth which, according to my grandad, gave the impression that he 'would tear you up if you troubled him'. My grandad had chuckled and said in his home-only Jamaican language 'Yu si his teet dem?' And he had gently pulled back the top lip of the friendly little puppy. 'Yu see how dem sharp like any file?'

Looking on, my grandma and I, both leaning forward and supporting ourselves on slightly bended knees, had studied the set of sharp little teeth and keenly searched for signs of tearing-up abilities – a major requisite for a guard dog. My grandad, businessman and the self-appointed expert on dogs and their teeth, continued. 'Yes man, a dawg wid teet like dhoes dwoon mek joke wid robbas. Once dey whoal aan to a man's shin, dey doan let go easy. Yu have to shake him off wid a blow or yu haf fi give up and calm down til him decide to let yu go.' He had produced another of his low throaty chuckles while he glanced at my grandma for her nod of agreement. She meanwhile had looked on with a hard to read expression on her face and murmured softly that she was doubtful a dog that size could do any damage to a determined robber.

But finally in an optimistic tone she had added 'A houpe your opinion betta dan mine Sam'. Then swiftly retreating from the subject, she said breezily 'Come Cass. Come an help yu granmadda shell some peas for her peas soup'. And hand in hand we had left my grandad there admiring Tearup and his grinning teeth while she softly hummed her favourite hymn 'Rock of ages cleft for me...' A song which always seemed to indicate the end of any argument or discussion.

Now her voice takes on a wistful note as she reflects on the past 'Your granfadda was a dawg expert. Or so he believed" she adds with a chuckle in her voice. "He did love his dawgs dem. Nobady was allowed to trouble them." And she reminds me of an incident. "Remember wen your uncle Winston did trouble one of dem? A had to send him home to his sister as it caused such a commotion when yu grandfadda come home and find the dawg run away to the village. Bwoy what a thing dat was."

I laughed as I remembered the incident after Uncle Winston had smacked the dog for eating my chicken's first ever egg.

Apart from Tearup the Terrible, there was also Mutt and Jeff, a pair of massive dogs, aptly named after two troublesome cartoon characters from the colour supplement of the Sunday newspaper. And last but not least, there was Busta, the big bulldog with the fearsome features and gruesome growl. He had been named after one of our Ministers of Parliament as, according to my grandfather, "He was handsome and strong, and didn't stand for any foolishness".

It was the fierceness of Busta's appearance and bark which

had made it necessary for the sign to be hurriedly painted and displayed at the entrance to the property. And since he was at the time, a lone dog, he was bequeathed some lieutenants in the form of Mutt and Jeff, and later Tearup, to help him with his 'tearing-up duties'. These additions also solved one of the grammatical errors on the sign which read 'BE-WARE OF THE DOGS'

I mention Busta and my gran laughs and says "Dey would ave lack up your granfadda if dey know dat he name one of his dawgs afta the Prime Minista". "Only him", she muses. And she settles back in her chair enjoying the memory.

So, accompanied by my four-legged friends, I complete my daily inspection of the gardens and check on the progress of the plants, the opening of buds, the too-slow ripening of the cherries and the overnight windfall of large silky-skinned avocados which lie green and shiny in the long dew-laden, but razor-sharp grass which grew at the base of the tall and forever fruitful tree. I fill the skirt of my nightdress and then trudge quietly back into the still sleeping house. My treasured English bedroom slippers, as usual, are heavy with fresh morning dew.

My gran kisses her teeth noisily and good-naturedly and said 'You and yu bedroom slippers. Anytime yu parents send you one a dem pretty shoes you always wanted to wear dem outside. To school. To church. Anywhere and everywhere.' She laughs at the memory. 'A had such a trouble stapping you.' And we laugh together as she concludes 'Yu could be so troublesome.'

But the day cannot begin until breakfast is eaten.

And my grandma's breakfasts were legendary!

'Yes dear, A used to do big a breakfast as some of the workers

use to eat here instead of at dere house. Miss Vie use to take it down to dem where they work in the fields.'

In any one week, the breakfast choices were endless and could include: Fried plantains, plantain fritters, fried sweet potatoes, callaloo, callaloo mixed with onions and bird peppers, Callaloo and salt fish fritters, Eggs with large unbroken yellow yolks, Soft warm hard-dough bread with a crumbly crust and lashings of yellow butter. And as if that wasn't enough, there was always a choice of piping hot, refreshing, Circe tea or freshly grated, milky, home grown cocoa, and grated banana porridge or hominy, made with succulent home-grown corn kernels and milk. But it was the final offering, the hot egg punch, a delicacy made just for the family, which was the most exciting breakfast fare. The delicious smelling yellow mixture which according to my grandma contained 'just a tip of rum' - a regular statement that was hard to believe as sometimes the heady smell, not to mention the warm and intoxicating taste, softened and disguised by mounds of yellow bubbles, affected my body as if a lot more than just 'a tip' of Jamaica's finest had been added.

Each morning, I dutifully drank the yellow concoction, while my grandmother highlighted the medicinal properties and intimated that if I refused any I would fail to thrive and not be good for anything; exhortations and mild threats which were to my mind, unnecessary. The heavy (but not too thick) warm, milky liquid laden with the magic elixir, together with great pinches of freshly grated nutmeg, copious beaten-to-death-eggs, lashings of milk freshly squeezed from the cow, was irresistible in smell and taste to children and adults alike. And even after the drink had been consumed, the yellow froth still had to be extracted from the pineapple decorated shot glasses, just deep enough to accommodate busy tongues - but only after the adults had turned their backs.

'I know you used to lick your glass out.' I can't help staring at her in surprise. *'But A neva badda to say anyting to you,* she continues, eyes twinkling, *So long as you neva lick it out in public!'*

And the effects of all this deliciousness? Maybe it was my over-active imagination, but I am almost certain that on many occasions after consuming this innocent-looking and comforting beverage, my movements down the drive to school would suddenly seem brisker than usual, my grandad's trademark, purposeful saunter across the lawn would display a slower and bouncier rhythm, and even my grandma's wave to our departing backs would appear to be just a little bit too enthusiastic. So today like all the other days before, I tuck into my feast without much encouragement as Grandma reminds me that "A good breakfast sets you up for the day'. And with today being the first day of my summer holiday from Flaxman All Age School, I just knew that it was going to be an extra special day.

Breakfast over and my gran says 'Go to the shop for me dear.'

'Why grandma?'

'Chile! Why is it you can't do anything without asking a question?'

After a pause, she says 'Just get out of your judging clothes. A don't want people to tink A don't look afta you for yu parents. Put something decent on. An hurry up'.

A smile flickers across her face, while her chin suddenly juts out playfully in my direction, leaving me in no doubt that an exciting announcement is about to be made. With winged feet, I fly away, leap out of my casual clothes and into my favourites – my red Scottish check trousers and my white t-shirt, the one with the man and woman doing something called skiing, right down the middle of it. Then I'm back beside her. Eager.

'Ready!' I announce as I leap into the kitchen and then stand steadily on both feet.

'What?' she wheels around, surprised. is how you can fly round so fast when you want to chile?'

'Because you sai…' I began.

'Never mind with yo long story. A want you to go to the shop quick for me as I want some sugar, butter and flour to do some baking.'

Baking? Baking! This is going to be the best of days!

'What're you baking today, gran?' I ask.

'Child why you so fass? Why you muss know every earthly ting?' She smiles at me, 'A want to bake some cakes if yu mus know.'

'Yes!' I say as my feet go into involuntary dancing mode while my arms try to reach themselves around her waist. As usual she tries to shrug me off in an uncaring fashion, and tries to adopt a mock crossness on her lovely soft face as she says

'Pickney why you doan leave me alone?' Followed by an exasperated 'Chuh!', which is like saying 'God!' but is forbidden in a God-fearing island.

I pause in my reflections to ask her if she still bakes.

'Yes dear. In fac I have a cake, I'm going to get it now. A bake it for yu yesterday.'

A special joy always used to descend on the farm whenever my Grandma, was in a cake-baking mood. It was a time of celebration for everyone. For me, for my grandad Mass Sam, for the farm workers, and for any visitor who happened to drop in unexpectedly after unendingly bawling 'Please hole the Dawg' from the distant gate with the 'Bad Dog' sign. And I also used to think it strange how many of our employees would find a reason to pop up to the house on my granma's baking days 'For some cool water, Miss Walker' they'd say, or 'To report something, Mistress O', and then in a surprised voice exclaim 'Oh yu baking today den, Mistress?' they'd ask nonchalantly while they eyed the activity in the kitchen and sniffed the resulting aroma.

They too, seemed to be aware that my gran produced the best tasting cakes in Jamaica, and they were always willing to try some samples while repeating between mouthfuls of the still warm, yellow and light brown concoctions, 'Tank you Miss Walker', or 'Tank you mistress' or 'Mmm this is good' followed in most cases by 'A could eat dis all day'.

And of course, buoyed up with all these compliments they would be rewarded with another sample. And maybe even a cool drink of sorrel which lay chilling in the huge American fridge. The one that I was always happy to open and close, as often as possible; once almost shutting my head in it while trying to see the magical light come on and go off. Did it or didn't it go off was the unending mystery. One of my grandma's speciality was a rich rum and plum cake, always bursting with - yes - rum and plum! This cake was my grandad's favourite too and I had heard him bafflingly say in between chews,

'Olga... there is more fruit... and rum... in dis cake... than cake'

But he would still quickly eat up to three slices one after the other.

'Gran d'you still make those drunken cakes?'

She chuckles and answers 'Yes mi dear. A still make dem for your aunties and uncles in Ocho.' She continues, 'Bwoy your grandfadda did love his cake. A had to hide dem if A wanted him to eat his dinna' she laughs. 'An as fa you and Errol!' and she raises her eyes heaven-wards, 'Every time I look at de cake I could see where a little bit nibble off or cut off. You two. A pair of trouble!' And she laughs again.

On other occasions, she made small round Greata cakes which would emerge from the oven with milk infused melt-in-the-mouth coconut, tightly packed into deep crinkly edged, crumbly pastry cases. But if she wasn't feeling too creative or if she was tired, she would just make a sponge cake. But these would never be like sponge cakes from the shop in Ocho Rios, these would be mouthwatering delicacies into which huge amounts of large, freshly laid eggs, from our own hens, were beaten and deposited to create their super sponginess. I would always gleefully contribute to the egg-beating ceremony with my favourite kitchen gadget - the wooden handled egg whisk specially made for its big glass jug. With professional manipulation resulting in furious rotations I would bring the recumbent eggs to supreme frothiness.

'Bwoy, you used to love helping me in the kitchen, Cass'.

She pauses, then asks

'Do yu still love cooking, dear?' she asks.

'Sometimes' I reply. 'I used to make rock cakes for my dad every Saturday when I went to England but I have a feeling that he only ate them to keep me happy'. I chuckle with the memory of him trying to get a grip on the big flat amorphously-shaped biscuits before chewing them with what seemed to be an extraordinary amount of effort for such a small morsel. But what had convinced me of their perfection was his constant murmurings of 'Mm, mm' as he chewed.

'Did your motha teach you to cook?'

'No gran. You taught me.'

I now remember how the magical jug of air would be gently folded into the cake mixture and in time would create cakes of the richest golden colour, and more than four times their original uncooked size. And their consistency! So light and fluffy that you felt you daren't leave your slice for long on the plate in case it floated out of your reach. So always best to eat it very quickly, and while it was still piping hot and dangerous! But my gran's best ever baking days were when she decided to do, not one or another type of cake, but all of these concoctions on the same day! And today, the first day of my school holiday, would be one of those days. So now to the shop! Excited and eager, I watch as she counts out the shiny coins and then adds the very large penny to the pile. I listen as she explains that she has fruits soaking in rum and needs the ingredients urgently. No sir! I don't need to be told about 'not letting the grass grow under my feet' which I know means 'don't take a long time'. I was happy to get to the shops and back in no time.

No, today was not a day for dawdling and sight-seeing. Not a time for playing with grass seeds or handling interesting insects that when touched by a small and curious forefinger can recoil and transform themselves into the shape and size of a fat pea. Or for bothering with leaves that have razor spikes, which if touched with a twig might suddenly snap shut and remain so for longer than one can wait. Nor even a day for playing dancing games with friends one might meet along the way. No. Today was an important day. Not an everyday sort of a day. It was going to be a cake-baking, cake-eating day!

So, with the shopping money safely secured in one of my gran's special starched, white, lace-trimmed church handkerchiefs, I set off on my journey, very aware of the big penny which sits underneath all the other smaller coins. The large brown coin which carries the picture of a lady who my gran says is called Britannia, and who now carries the promise of some delicious sweets! Either four scrumptiouus Mint Balls or four long-lasting and supersuckable Paradise Plums, or even two of each of some other mouth-wateringly good sweets. Spending my big penny was always the highlight of my shopping trips!

'A couldn't send you to the shap widout yu penny' she says with a chuckle. 'Dats de only reason yu enjoy going to the shap. No adder reason, I know.'

In a tearing hurry, I sped away from my home which stands on the gently-sloping hill, surrounded by lawns and geometrically shaped flowerbeds. Away from the confidently square house with its crisp blue wooden trim and its blue and white striped awnings shading the large deep veranda, and past the long empty garage with its now open, up and over metal door which stands at the beginning of our L- shaped drive. The place where at the end of each day on his return home from his business in Tower Isles, my grandad parks his ever-changing styles of American cars. The place which is the temporary daytime resting place for the occasional delivery van or visitor's cars and even, on one memorable occasion, served as the parking space for my aunt's Rolls Royce on her wedding day.

Now I run down the gentle slope of the drive as if pursued by bad dogs. Past the rows of shiny leaved dwarf orange trees, specially bred by my grandad. On past the dense banana walk with its dark mysterious interior. And then finally I clamber up and over the imposing iron gates with its chain and bolt combination. Now I am going past the cemetery, which, under strict instructions from my grandma is out of bounds. That edict was thrown down after I had on one too many occasions wandered in to funerals uninvited, and had suffered a spate of nightmares which had left everyone bewildered and worried. When my gran had solved the mystery of the source of my nightmares, she had not only banned me from entering the gates of this amenity which ran alongside one section of our land, but had threateningly wagged a stiff forefinger in my face, which was frighteningly close to her furious features, and bellowed, 'Dat place is dead to you, you hear me Cassandra?'

So now, with her voice ringing in my ears, and the money clutched tightly in my hand, I avert my face from the forbidden place and with a most urgent speed, hurry towards the shop.

'Yes,' recalls my gran 'A had to waan yu about dat cemetery'. 'What business yu did have looking at dead people who yu

didn't know?' 'Yu was just faas.' She added, 'If you don't know people when dey living an den you a look at dem when dey dead, you bound to have nightmares! A was glad when A fine out what yu been up to.' She shakes her head ruefully and continues, almost to herself, *'Yu fadda was going to come back from England when he hear yu was behaving like dat. Troublesome chile!'* she concludes as she chucks her chin at me playfully.

Now past the forbidden cemetery, I turn left onto the Content Road of which my grandad had warned me 'Yu should mind how yu walk along dat road Cassie. Is a very busy road full of dangerous mad men driving cars that they can't control!'

But I know this road 'like the back of my hands' as the big people said. I can walk along it blindfolded. Anyway, at my last car-counting exercise from the veranda, I only counted three cars in one hour. There is no danger. I hurry along it confidently but with urgency. Today, even a big black sack of ants hanging, like a block of concrete from the misshapen trunk of a dying tree, cannot hold my attention for too long. Well, only long enough to count one hundred of the occupants. Fascinated, I watch them and marvel – not for the first time - at how, with their large tops and huge bottoms almost separated by a miniscule waist, they resemble miniature school children wearing excruciatingly tightly-belted red school uniforms.

Now I am passing Miss Stanley's empty cave and I remember not only her flowing white, wavy hair but also her face all embellished with what people said were freckles, but which to me seemed as if someone had been preparing her face for a 'Join the Dots' game. Day after day she would sit in her cave and before you even saw her you could hear the sound of breaking rocks, which my grandad said was for the road constructors.

Do you remember Miss Stanley granma?' I ask.

'Yes dear. She was a nice woman.' She pauses then explains, 'She use to be rich in her younger days, but people said dat when her husband died, his family slowly took away her money. She ended up breaking rocks for a living well into her old age. A very sad story my dear' she says in a low voice as she shakes her head slowly from side to side.

As I walk past the cave where she worked I ponder on how one day she was here working and by the next day she was gone forever; her pile of rocks sitting just where she'd left them. And I recall how on one of her working days, Miss Stanley, after thanking and blessing my grandma for the food parcel she had sent, had given me an open-mouthed smile of gratitude and I had noted with sudden alarm and shock, that like a baby, Miss Stanley hadn't any teeth. All that she revealed inside that openmouthed smile were firm looking pink gums which she expertly used to demolish the fried dumplings and saltfish that my gran had sent for her.

As if woken from a dream I now hear the insistent voice of my grandmother saying, "Cassy don't let the grass grow under your feet". This had the effect of lengthening my skips as I imagined her stern expression, but also the hot delicious cakes emerging from the oven. Mmm. The cake vision whirls tantalisingly in my head and I urge myself forward. I skip and skip and skip on through the quietest part of the road - the too-cool part with its dark looming hills on either side where the thick tangled ropes of Wis hang down like the tails of enormous seated monsters. Past the large old overhanging trees which on most other days but strangely not today, have a life of their own inside their big heads of dark shiny leaves. I hurry through the silence, as if for the first time, and the sunless semi-darkness creates in me an unusual feeling of unease. So that's why I skip with particular urgency around the next bend and into what I know will be sunlight. And that is when I see the stranger.

'Oh God!' exclaimed my gran. 'My poor little Cassie.'

This man, I note in an instant, is dressed in very memorable clothes and has a long, dark, hard-looking face. A blade of long grass protrudes from his mouth while his eyes look straight across the road and off unseeing into the distance. I realise with alarm and trepidation that he is definitely not what we have been warned about when the subject of strangers had been discussed. So, he can't be a bad stranger, I think.

I wonder if he has seen me. I plan to walk past him, at a distance, unseen. Now my heart is beating fast and loud and there is a weak hungry feeling in my stomach.

Wanting to appear unafraid I force my legs to continue skipping while I try to make them travel diagonally and away from the man. Skip, skip, skip. Harder, harder, harder I urge them on and I try to believe that he is not there. That he has not seen me. Skip, skip, skip. Soon I will have gone past him. Past his aloneness, and past his silence. I hold my breath and look straight ahead of me and into the distance, while I wonder about the type of stranger that he is. No, he is not the kind of stranger that parents with wild eyes and wagging fingers warn their children about. He isn't a Sweetie Man. No, he isn't. He can't be. Because he is not white. He isn't the kind of 'stranger wearing sun glasses'. The type who is known by all children to sit in big, dark-windowed cars, silently waiting for lone children. The kind who will call you in a too friendly American voice to 'Come and get a sweet little girl' or 'little boy', and then who will grab you and drive you away forever to use your heart to make new kidcatching sweets. The kind that might miss you as he tried to grab you. The one you could duck from. Or run into someone's house from. No. This man is different. He can't drive me away.

So why is my heart racing so noisily? He is a black man. So he can't be a bad man, I tell myself. I decide to just skip unnoticed past him. Skip, skip, skip while my heart beats loudly. Lub dub. Lub dub. Lub dub. I scroll through my memory. Have I seen him before in the shop? No. Have I seen him before in church? No. He is a stranger. Sitting as if he belongs here. I decide that I do not like him, or his silence. Or his face, which I have seen in just one glance. A face which I know looks like a large old bone discarded by one of our dogs. A bone that has been left out in the sun for a very long time. A hungry face. *'Dirty scoundrel splutters my gran. Ool convict.'*

He is out of place here, where when the cool evening breeze replaces the fierce midday sun, people congregate with vessels to fetch water. A meeting place of fun and laughter. Where children, accompanied by their parents, come to have water fights after a hot day. Where boys with their tops off, have water-drinking competitions that make their uncovered bellies bulge dangerously as the water swishes noisily around inside them as they leap about. Now the stranger sits on the parapet as still and silent as a rock. Yes, one more skip and I will be safe. But no! There is an awful roaring from his direction. My head grows to an enormous size and I am instantly rooted to the spot. The roar translates into words that say, 'Come here likkle girl'. *'God have mercy!' exclaims my gran as she looks at me with pity.*

I breathe in suddenly while invisible ropes hold me rooted to the spot. My heart is beating with a faster and louder lub-dub, lub-dub, lub-dub. And a voice like a needle on a scratched vinyl record adds to the nightmare and says again and again and again 'Run away… run away… run away'. But still I stand immobile under the blazing sun as I try to understand the words of the stranger and command my reluctant feet to run away from the nightmare. And as the shimmering heat from the hot tar engulfs me, I hear another voice. A strange trembling voice, and it says 'No!' quite firmly, and immediately releases an avalanche which dislodges huge jagged rocks which creates a dreadful sound. They rush at me with hurtling speed, and land with a force which seems to lift me off my feet and leaves me weightless in the air. Each rock is a word spoken in a voice deep, low and full of menace and promise. They say 'Come here! Or a gwine cut off yu neck.'

'Jesus have mercy!' gasps my gran as if she has never heard these words said before, and her face is contorted in pain as she stares hard into my frightened child's face.

I gasp in horror as each word is fired from the weapon of his cruel mouth leaving me stunned and breathless from the onslaught. A weakness descends on me. A feeling of hopelessness overwhelms me as my body seems to collapse from within, and as a never-ending scream ricochets inside my head. I stand still and helpless, staring unblinkingly at the long, long road ahead, while my mouth poises itself to raise the alarm. But it won't. It can't. It is frozen, and my throat lies dry and soundless and my lungs wait in anticipation of the large intake of breath. But it waits in vain for the crucial gasp to arrive; the gasp of air which will aid in the making of that scream. A wild head-thrown-back scream like one I had witnessed issuing from someone confronted by a snarling dog. An earthshattering alarm that will signify my terror.

But there is no sound. No noise, like iron on iron ringing shrilly through the surrounding trees. No sound that will send flocks of birds soaring helter-skelter like an alarm, into the sky. A soaring which could be witnessed by men in nearby clearings and read as a sign of danger, causing someone to look up and wonder, and then maybe run to my rescue. There is just the silence of frozen time, immobile trees and noiseless birds. And me.

Trapped and rigid with a new feeling. Terror.

My gran is no longer eating but is watching me with horror in her eyes as if it has all just happened yesterday.

Then like a marionette in slow and petrified motion, I turn, and move towards the stranger. Move across the interminable wide hot asphalted abyss which divides us.

And as I slowly tread towards my doom, I hear the voice.

'Honestly granma, it was like your voice saying "Don't look at his face Cassie, for God's sake don't look at his face"'.

'Yes, it was God, my dear' she says raising her eyes in a silent thanks to heaven.

So, I look ahead, and past his face. I walk towards what I know now is a Sweetie man disguised as a black man. I stand in front and slightly to his left and I think of Daniel in the lion's den. I am to be eaten. About to replace the waggling straw being pulverised by what I know are giant jagged teeth in his boney gyrating jaws.

A sharp movement causes me to jump and I look down to see long, bony claw-like fingers stretched out in front of me. They are ashen and gnarled, just like his huge ugly nails which seem to have been baked. He flicks them suddenly with a dry and rasping impatient click. Right under my nose. And once again, I flinch as I stare down at the cruel claws which have created the sound. What? I do not understand their command. I fail to respond. And then his talons dive down towards my waist, where my hands, small and quivering, sit supporting each other. There is a sudden snatching movement, and my handkerchief is in his claws. I stand motionless and helpless, and from the edge of my eyes I saw his hands pull and tug and wrench and grapple with the firm knots tied by my grandmother.

'Dat dirty tief!' spits my granma suddenly. 'If A did come up on im just den yu si! A would have paan a piece a stick and den ee wouldn't lef wid hand to open handkerchief.' She pauses before spitting out the word 'Rabba!' before she breathes a deep sigh of frustration at being thwarted in getting her hands on the thief.

So, I'm standing in what I feel is the lion's den. Seeped in terror. Inside, I pray, like Daniel in the story, to be rescued.

'Poor ting' says my grandma. 'Go on darling.'

'Well...I wet myself while I stood in front of him you know

grandma? That's how terrified I was.'

'My Gad Cass! A didn't know all dat happen to you dear. My poor little Cassie' and she shakes her head ruefully.

Down, down, down it came as I stood captive in front of the stranger. And it seeps silently through my pink slippers and into the melting heat of the asphalted road. And disappears, leaving no evidence of my terror.

Now suddenly, the wizened dusty claws, still holding my handkerchief, rises up to my face. He shakes it again more violently, and like a dazed puppet I reach up and hold it, while a strange feeling of relief sweeps over me.

Still frozen, I stand there, obediently waiting. Then his talons are once again moving in front of my face. I flinch as his claws open and close several times like the wings of a huge dusty bird. They flick dismissively, and I gulp in disbelief.

What? What does he want? He flicks again. Away. Away. I can go away? I can go away! Now comes the roaring in my head. But just in time, I remember the voice, and I stop myself from looking at his face. Stop myself from saying in a small and grateful voice 'Thank you'.

'Run yu hear mi dear,' says my gran, and I know she's there with me reliving the horror.

My heart pounds out an erratic tune as I turn and will my leaden legs to run away. Run away! Run away! Run away! I urge them, but they fail. So stiffly, like a rusty puppet, I walk away. Further and further. Faster and faster. Away from the Stranger. And still terrified, I wait for the sudden touch of his bony, blistered fingers on my frightened neck.

'Lawd Jesus' breathes my gran. I pause, and we acknowledge simultaneously, our terror, and relief...

At the next bend in the road, with my heart pounding like a drum, my legs begin to move faster and faster, and I run and run and run, for my life.

'Thank God you get away.' She raises her eyes and hands to heaven and her mouth is moving in what I know is a silent prayer of thanks, all these years later.

Now in the sanctuary of the shop the latest number one tune screams out from the juke box.

Oh Carol, I am but a fool.

Darling I love you.

Though you treat me cruel.

It is my favourite song and it comforts me, while the shop cloaks me in all its warmth and familiarity. It is a meeting place for everyone. Mothers, children, and men of all ages. And sometimes even dogs. And my arrival coincides with a debate related to the latter.

In Jamaica, everyone, regardless of age know the rule about dogs inside buildings with humans. It is not allowed. And so its eviction follows the usual pattern, starting with the usual question.

'Wha da dawg a do in ear?' This is said by a customer whose voice conveys a huge dose of alarm, heavily sprinkled with a thick coating of disgust. Next comes a chorus of other voices, all equally alarmed and offended 'Dawg'?

Now all chatter and noise ceases as if to signify the presence of a wild animal instead of a curious, innocent, lost dog being at large. The attention of every customer is now trained on the poor unfortunate creature, who has by now sensed that he is an unwelcome visitor. Voices of outrage begin to swell.

'But wait!' someone sarcastically observes, 'Dawg a shap now?'

Then another voice gets in on the act and addresses the shopkeeper 'But Bennet, you caan have dawg inna yu shap a rub up rub up wid people'.

Next, there's a command from someone else 'Hey! Smaddy, tek out dis dawg man!'

And before long, another voice with the obligatory expression of disgust, 'Choo!' followed by a kissing of teeth sounding like fish plonked in hot oil.

Then a decisive statement from someone else "Me na shap nowhere whe dawg a stroll bout like dem own de shap".

This creates a ripple of laughter, and someone else agrees with a long string of nasal sounding "Eee-eh" followed by a long, almost never-ending kissing of their teeth.

The background comments about the dog continue, and before long someone else adds to the commentary with a loud 'Yes, an a smell-up smell-up whey people haf fe buy, like him have money.'

This statement elicits another loud burst of laughter. *My gran is laughing at the images being conjured up, and it breaks the tension we're both feeling. She compliments me with*

'Cass A didn't know yu could speak Jamaican. A will have to tell everbady how me English granddata funny' she laughs.

While these objections to the dog are being voiced, children, myself included, are warily glancing at it and trying to keep our distance. Our fears gives a new participant a reason why the dog should be immediately ejected. 'Look man,' he says, 'Yu caan see say the pickney dem fraid a de dawg?'

Before long a new voice trying to bring matters to a speedy end asks authoritatively

'Is whose dawg dis?'

There is a pause before a subdued response of 'Is my dawg' comes from the domino-playing area, whereupon many voices loudly demand that he should 'Tek de dawg out man!'

In turn, the owner's testy response is, 'But a no me bring him ya! A him falla me from mi yard.'

And above the shower of laughter which ensues, someone says 'Well if yu dawg love you so much, den yu haf fi stay wid im ina yu house, man. Yu caan mek him come in a de shop a stroll roun, stroll roun, wid decent people.'

There are murmurs of 'Is true dat' followed by 'Yu caan have dawg a eggs up ina de shap like im is smaddy!'

This is followed by a loud and prolonged 'Chhhh!' which emits the hiss of onions being thrown into the oil, alongside the fish.

My gran is laughing silently as I continue with the story.

The original enquirer then causes a roar of laughter when he asks the owner. "Yu dawg can play domino?" And as the laughter subsides he begins speaking to the dog as if it too speaks and understands English

'Dawg,' he begins, bending down to face the dog and waving his forefinger 'Stay outside where yu belang. Doon't let me si yu in ere again a eggs up yuself wid people.' Then finally 'Yu hear me dawg?'

The dog, bearing a couldn't care less expression on its face, warily edges its way outside for some peace and quiet; and as always, someone concludes the event with 'Dutty eggsup Dawg!' followed by a long dismissive kissing of teeth.

My gran chuckles and then says after a long pause, 'My dear, A jus so glad yu reach the shap. Thank you Jesus!'

Dog crisis over, I make my way towards the display of sweets lying tantalisingly under the huge domed glass counter, while behind me the mothers shop and gossip, and the old men, whom my grandad laughingly call 'old drunkards', play loud dominoes. With my hands supported by slightly bent knees, I gaze admiringly at the sweets, and as I drink in their colours, their shapes and their promised flavours, the face of the robber evaporates. First, I examine the oval shaped, pink and white striped Paradise Plums which I know taste of the juices of cherries and star apples. Then I drag my gaze to the fat and perfectly rounded Mint Balls with their jaunty red and white beachball stripes, and which taste through and through of a sweet but minty flavour which can be savoured for a long time if not too quickly demolished by over-eager teeth.

Then peering to the back of the glass dome, I can see nestling amongst an array of others which fail to hold my interest, the long-lasting chewy ones whose name but not their qualities, momentarily escapes me. Dark brown and concealed in their slightly oily looking paper, they lie quietly and mysteriously, waiting to be chosen. I know that the flat square shapes, are made of crunchy coconut flavoured with ginger and cinnamon, tightly bound together with chewy teeth-gripping black molasses and dark brown demerara sugar. They beckon me to buy them. To own them. To eat them. To demolish them slowly with a glass of milk. But just two of these will cost me my whole penny, so I make my decision and place my order.

'Two Mint Balls and two Paradise Plums please Mr. Bennet' I say and continue to stare and salivate, briefly pausing in my admiration to reach up and deliver my handkerchief into the big capable outstretched right hand of the shopkeeper.

Above my head I can hear the rustle of the paper parcels being made for the sugar and the flour, and I know that Mr. Bennet is also making a long brown paper cone, like a miniature party hat, for my sweets. There is a pause and I hear him speaking some unexpected words.

'But Miss Cass, he chuckles, 'Yu only have a penny in yu kerchief.'

I drag my eyes upwards and stare at him in disbelief and alarm as I suddenly remember the day I had lost some money when I had been collecting leaves of different sizes, and on discarding them, had unwittingly thrown away the tenshilling note; on the one and only occasion that my grandma had not wrapped the shopping money in a handkerchief. On my return home I had tearfully related my misfortune to her, highlighting how kind Mr. Bennet had still given me the shopping. She had angrily referred to the loss as 'My big ten-shilling note' and admonished me for being careless. But I was very surprised when she had retrieved a strange piece of paper bearing Mr. Bennet's handwriting which revealed to me that the bill and the cost of my sweets would still have to be paid for. The sucking and slurping of my third Paradise Plum had instantly ceased.

My Gran laughs and murmurs

'Ah Mr. Bennet, she says wistfully, He is a very kind man. Dat man, he would neva see anyone go hungry. He would always let them owe him. A good and decent family. Dey still live in the house but his children run the shap now. He would love to see you.' She pauses. 'Anyway, Go on Cass.'

As his smiling face looks kindly down at me from a great height I say with some certainty

'No, my granma put all the money in the handkerchief.'

'You sure yu didn't lose it Miss Cass' he asks with a smile.

'No Mr. Bennet, I.... I.... I'.

And then I remembered. How the man had snatched and scrabbled with the nice clean handkerchief. Then how it had been placed still knotted into my shaking hands. And suddenly the realisation came. I had met a thief!

Now the fear and the terror overwhelms me and the colours and shapes of the sweets all blur into one. The noisy shop began to spin as a high-pitched screaming resounds in my ears. And the stranger is beside me and the screams get louder and louder. He holds me by the shoulders and I look up into the face of Mr. Bennet. He is hushing me. Asking me questions. The people are all silent and looking at me with sympathy. And I feel, as the crash of the last dominoes explode in the distance, that they're waiting on me. Waiting for my story.

My halting words coalesce with my loud pitiful mewings as a magical glass of sugar and water - the best balm for distress, woes and wounds of a Jamaican child - is placed into, and cupped by my trembling hands. This concoction, to a foreigner, would appear to be just plain water. Water - magically transformed in an instant by the addition of a spoonful or two of sparkling rich soft brown sugar. The silky sweetness of the potion quickly flows through me after two quick gulps, and magically I begin to haltingly recall the ordeal which happened in broad daylight just a few minutes beyond the bend in the road.

I tell them of the lone man sitting there. Calling me. Threatening me. Of his shocking words, his threatening fingers, his stone like face, and each description creates a hurricane of rage amongst the customers. Mr. Bennet, his long biscuit-coloured face and huge eyes of disbelief asks, 'What he said?'

As I repeat the words 'Come here likkle girl or a gwine cut off your neck' there is again, a communal intake of breath, and when they exhale, there is another thunderstorm of outrage and disbelief. The people's roaring anger seems to find refuge in new utterances. Bad words shoot around like jagged pieces of metal all directed at the unknown man.

Dire threats are made on his life. And the name of God is repeated like an incantation from all the mouths around me, while their eyes look in the direction of heaven. I glance up and see the terrified eyes of a group of women looking down on me, and one says in a voice of wonder and despair 'Lord what's happening to our country?' And then someone else cries 'Is what we have in our midst?' And adds, 'Lawd deliva us from evil'. Some people beside her send their arms, open-palmed, shooting into the sky in a begging fashion while they say in a prayer-like voice and with their eyes closed, 'Lawd deliva us from evil' Then from the far end of the shop, a lone voice in high pitched tone begs 'Lord help us here in Jamaica'. And from the open doorway, yet another voice hoarse with anger, bellows 'Lord help us cause we have John Crows living in our midst!'

But suddenly the mood changes from one of begging to one of intent as someone through bared teeth and exhibiting contorted grimaces, vows loudly that she will 'Rip de dutty tief from head to toe ef A catch him near one of mi pickney"'. Her eyes roll dramatically as a chorus of voices join hers with solutions.

'Murder him'.

'Hang him'.

And then a more conciliatory but strident 'Lack im up'.

But it quickly reverts back to violent imagery when someone adds 'Batter him senseless, man'.

Other voices add unrepeatable adjectives which are only heard by forgotten children who sit quietly and invisibly in the vicinity of adults late at nights. The reaction of the people slowly reveals to me the seriousness of the robber's actions as everyone agrees that 'He is a 'dutty naiga, a dutty tief', and that 'Im hafi go to prison ar hang!' And a woman's voice adds 'One way or anada, we haf to mek sure im is kept away from decent people's children.'

My gran says, 'The whole district was very cut up about the whole thing.' 'Nothing like dat ever happen here before'.

As the promise of further dire retributions are spelt out, someone murmurs ominously 'If we catch him yu si? No tree high enough to hang im fram.' There is a responsive murmur of 'A tell yu!' I whimper and sip my pacifier while the domino playing old men in the far corner fume and growl in lowered tones. And from time to time, individuals, some still holding their domino pieces, thrust their arms violently into the air while making vile oaths and threats to the unseen robber.

One man say he would 'Catch him, tie him up and then tear him limb from blasted limb for troubling a likkle girl', while another person after slamming down a domino with extreme force said, When I finish wid im he won't be able to see ar even talk eva again.' Then with a deep mirthless chuckle, one of the players add that he hoped the robber already had children because 'When I finish wid im yu si, he nat going to be hable to av any'. Surprisingly, the statement creates laughter, and he concludes dramatically, while raising his right hand and stating in the tone of a priest making a promise, 'A true! As God is mi witness!'

I sip my drink as the scale of horrific punishments rise. Another of the domino men adds one more to the list. 'If I catch him yu si,' he says slowly and deliberately 'A would a walk him barefoot, yes man, barefoot,' and adds for emphasis 'An slow, ova a whole heap a hat coal!' Adding with some relish, 'Yu know when the coal dem really hat an a shimma? Den!' This statement, together with his facial expressions and gestures summarising how the thief would walk over the coals, create such a strong picture in my mind that I snort involuntarily with laughter. The mood changes instantly. All eyes are now on me and they seem to stare with gratitude. With radiant smiles and nods they declare 'Look! She laughing!'

Then someone says 'Poor likkle ting'. And they smile with

relief at each other before returning their satisfied gaze to my tear-stained face.

New people appear and are surprised to find a drama unfurling in the middle of the day in their local grocery store. Some whisper loudly 'But no Miss Cass that?' Someone else says with surprise, 'But no Mrs. Walker gran-pickney dat?' What happen to har?' Another person murmurs 'Mr. Walker, im don't joke yu know!'

And another says menacingly 'Har granfadda gaan fine him yu know.' Then in the contemplative silence that ensues as their eyes linger on me, someone wanting to play his own part in the drama, says in a voice brimming with specialised knowledge, 'Dem no say Walka have gun?' Not a word is spoken but all eyes turn in his direction as he continues 'Ee gwan shoot dat dutty rabba.'

The eyes of his audience linger on the speaker before they turn to look at me as if for confirmation. I shrink within myself and silently ponder on this dramatic revelation.

I now glance at my grandmother for confirmation about the gun but she is engaged in securing a new slice of delicious cake, and the mystery remains unsolved and buried in the past.

As calm settles over the shop, Mr. Bennet suddenly instructs his wife, 'Lyn bring me mi long handled cutlass. A gwine tek Miss Cass home'.

She reaches under the counter and straightens up holding a fearsome slab of steel which brings a loud gasp followed by deathly silence from the crowd. Carefully she threads her way across the room towards her husband while holding the instrument as though it was a poisonous snake. The crowd parts, and we all stare almost reverentially at the smooth wooden handle firmly secured to the metal by large shiny studs, and at the long broad curved silver blade, which from the back to the front gradually decreases from a solid slab into a thin and dangerous-looking edge.

Taking the weapon as though greeting a friend, Mr. Bennet says breezily, 'Drink up Miss Cass; yu granmadda mus be wandering where you are.'

At the mention of my grandmother I quickly drain my glass, take his out-stretched hand, and we leave the crowded shop as loud angry voices instruct him to 'Chap dat damn robba if you fine him.'

And 'See if he can wrestle yu cutlass out a yu hand as yu chop im to pieces' advises another, adding after a pause 'An si if him still have Miss Cass money before you chap im up.' They all laugh uproariously at their jokes. Then smiling confidently Mr. Bennett parts with a 'Me gaan.' And we set off for Pleasant Farm.

"Bennet man? says my gran, He wasn't a man to play wid in his young days! He could be a bad man wen anyone confront him in his shap. Everybady did know dat he doan joake.' And she chuckles, a deep rumbling mirthless chuckle; in the same way that some of the people in the shop had chuckled on the day of the incident.

I'm eager to be home but as we near the corner, new fears crawl into my mind. Will we see the robber again? Will he call me again? Will Mr. Bennett be able to kill him? Now I cling even tighter to my protector, and he in turn, gives my hand a squeeze. We turn the corner and with eyes ahead of my face,

I scan the parapet. There is a sudden movement there. Once more, my legs refuse to move, and an empty feeling returns to the pit of my stomach. But horror of horror, Mr. Bennet hails someone and looks down at me, laughing, as I look up at him with terrified eyes.

'Don't worry yuself Miss Cass, he says. Is nat de bad man dat, Is some bwoy fram the shap. A know dem'. He calls out to the men 'Unno did fine de dutty naiga?'

'No sah.' they shout back. As we get closer, one of the young men adds 'Im mussi run wey afta him tek weh de likkle girl money.'

'Dutty tief!' spat Mr. Bennett.

'We was ready fi him, sah' One of the young men say and they all laugh again with that now familiar mirthless rumble. A threatening rumble of menace and danger as if from a hungry lion that has spotted its half-hidden prey and now feels pretty certain of its meal.

We set off once more on our journey and Mr Bennett, who has been looking closely at the undergrowth, suddenly swings his cutlass in the air and shouts in an angry voice 'Come out yu dutty naiga. Come out an face me.'

I look towards where he is staring, not knowing who or what I will see, and watch in horror as he brings his cutlass down sharply with a loud thwack onto a thick, tangled, human-shaped piece of undergrowth. I watch as the huge silver blade flashes from side to side with a rapid swish, swish, swish, slicing the tops from the plants and vines and maybe even the head of a hiding robber. Mr Bennet grins excitedly while shouting some of what I know are not nice words, and then as if he suddenly remembers my presence, glances sheepishly at me and says

'Miss Cass, A haf to mek a whole lot a noise to frighten that tiefing bad man. A haf to show im that a badder man than him is here with a damn blasted cutlass to cut off HIS blasted neck!' Yu andastan me Miss Cass?' And he laughs again as he gives the undergrowth a final whack.

My gran seems to be enjoying this detail about Mr. Bennet's show of bravado and her voice is heavy with admiration. 'Bennet, God Bless him fa lookin afta you'. I think of Mr Bennet with gratitude and realise that he was a Robin Hood type of hero. As if to confirm my thoughts my gran adds 'Not a real bad bad man', she explains 'but a bad man who do good things for good people.'

I look up at Mr. Bennet with his cutlass raised up to the sky like a warrior and in a flash I suddenly realise that I was holding the hand of the renowned 'Cutlass Bennet'! I had always thought the name belonged to someone whose first name was 'Cutlass'

My gran laughs out loud. 'Everybady, far and wide did know about Cutlass Bennet! From time immemorial, dat's one shap where rabbas walk far fram, since the day when Bennet chase one down the road wid his cutlass. People did say dat it was only God dat did help de dirty robba to escape wid his life.' She chuckles again and continues 'News spread far and fass my dear.' Then she sighs and adds with some feeling 'Dats why the dirty thief decided to rab you instead. Because he didn't have the courage to face Bennet and his cutlass, he rab a little eight year old girl!' She pauses before adding 'Hm, once a scoundrel, always a scoundrel'

Then home at last, and the gate to Pleasant Farm, hidden away in its abundance of foliage, creaks our arrival. *'And that's when I saw you coming through the bananawalk, you know granma. You looked really angry and I thought you were going to beat me.'*

'A was. A was worried. And A was going to beat you because A jus taut you was up at dat shap dancing wid your friends.' Then her eyes widen in disbelief as she continues, *'But is when A saw Mr. Bennet holding your hand dat A realised someting was wrong. A couldn't get to yu quick enough, dear. My poor little Cassie.'* And the love in her eyes is heartbreakingly clear.

'Oh grandma' I say, and I can't help reaching across to hug her in memory of that day.

Together, arm in arm, we walked back along the L shaped drive and I listened, mute and shaken, while their smudged voices rumbled softly above my head.

'As soon as Bennet told me the story, said my gran, A sent one of the boys wid a message to your grandad at Tower Isles and he was here quick, quick. He was as mad as anything. Said he'd heard from your uncle Buttley that a little red Ebow child was robbed, but not for one minute did he think it was you. Not until he got the message.' After a pause she said *'Dear Sam, God rest his soul'* and she looks off into the distance...

Later that day, my grandmother and I, dressed in hat and gloves like paper pattern models, waited for the arrival of my grandfather.

Soon we spot his sky blue fish tail American car snaking up the L shaped drive. As usual, my grandfather's daily welcome home party gathered. First the dogs doing their bottom-scraping, tail wagging dances, then the chickens – half flying half stumbling, then the peacocks with their showy struttings, followed by the forever hungry group of speckled guinea fowls, and lastly, not to be outdone even in their enforced absence – the cows in their distant pasture gave their lowing welcome. But much to their surprise, the entertainment was abruptly curtailed as we leapt into the still slow-moving car which then took a rapid circular turn and had them bemusedly scattering and squawking in all directions.

On an ordinary day this style of driving on the part of my grandad would have been termed by my grandmother, through taut lips, as recklessness, since it had narrowly missed a group of 'good laying-hens'. Following the near carnage, we had travelled at breakneck speed, back down the drive, flashing past orange trees heavily laden with fruits, a lone cherry tree festooned with blossoms and the promise at last of cherries, past the sign that said 'Be-Ware of Bad Dogs', and finally through the big iron gates - opened, just in time, by Alrick the big smiling boy, one of many who worked on our farm.

Now onto the Gale Road along which I had tearfully and fearfully travelled only two hours earlier. And as the scenery had flown backwards, my grandmother had narrated the events of the day in a serious monotone to her nodding husband while

I had listened, checking her story for accuracy, and marvelled at how it had sounded as if she had been there with me when I had met the bad man.

'Gran remember when you told grandad about the robber that day? You sounded as if you had been there with me you know'.

She smiles with a faraway look in her eyes and said, 'My dear, maybe A was. A had a funny feeling in my stomach from the moment yu had left the house. But A prayed and set my mind at rest. A knew dat God was with yu.'

Now instinctively I avert my face as we pass the cemetery and once on the now busy Content Road, my grandad in a rare state of anger, suddenly banged his fist on the steering wheel and spoke forcefully 'I pay enough taxes in this town, and I want to get something back for it. Dey have to catch dat rat...' But he stops as suddenly as he begun, after receiving what appeared to be a sharp movement from my gran's right elbow. From the safety of the plush leather seats which hug me, I peep fearfully just above the rim of the window, scanning the crowd for a man wearing a shirt decorated with red and yellow flowers.

Before long, the flashing yellow indicator arm shoots out and the purring car takes a sharp left turn. We proceed slowly up a crunchy white gravel drive that leads towards a large sprawling bungalow which sits alone in an oasis of green lawn punctuated at precise intervals by large hibiscus shrubs, all festooned in red flowers. After the first corner I see the chief of police, Mr. Roberts, dressed in his striking red and black uniform with matching peaked cap, smiling as he strides towards us. We emerge into the sunshine and he greets us with a friendly 'How-de-do' while offering his outstretched hand to my grandad, followed by 'Sam'. Then still smiling, he turns to my grandmother and shakes her ungloved hand while he bows and says in a softer mesmeric voice 'Mrs. Walker'. And then just before turning back to my grandad, almost as if he has suddenly remembered something, he looks down at me, displays a hint of a gold tooth as he chuckles and says 'Miss Cass'. Using the expected sing-song voice of children, I say 'Hello Mr. Roberts', as his hand gently bounces on my plaits.

We stroll towards the veranda and I can hear, against my will, my grandad and Mr. Roberts talk about the dryness of the land, the difficulties of their jobs and the spraying of crops. I try as hard as I can to adhere to the unwritten rule for every Jamaican child. 'Not to listen in to big people's conversations' - but in spite of my efforts, and above the noise of the crunchy white gravel, I still catch a few snatches of what they say. Words like 'criminal', 'Bad man' from Mr. Roberts, 'Catch him', and, 'Locked up for a long time' from my grandad. Their words sound angry and are dramatized by finger-stabbing gestures, while my grandmother who is walking behind them nods and issues low mournful murmurs through pursed lips.

We enter a large cool room and I am captivated by the magnificence of my surroundings. All the bad memories of the day instantly disappear. The room, one of the largest I had ever seen, was not the prison that I had anticipated. The one that had been implanted in our imaginations by the big boys at school. They, the reluctant students who had overstayed the school-leaving age deadline, and who had probably been threatened with being sent to a place like this, had often regaled us the smaller children as we walked home from school, with gory descriptions of the interior of this place at which we in turn had thrown askance glances from street level while we allowed our over-fertile imaginations to run amok.

So while the adults, at a distance, spoke in hushed tones, I scanned my surroundings and found that there were no heavy chains, no hooks or manacles, no whips, and definitely no skeletons, and nor were there any kerosene lamps or wooden torches wrapped in oily rags as depicted in the American comics such boys devoured. Instead, the room was brilliantly lit by a chandelier bearing a whole nest of light bulbs which resembled the big tree that stood in the Content Road cemetery and at night flashed with the winking lights of peenie wallies - or 'fireflies', as my teacher had once corrected us in a crisp English accent. This object of beauty bathed the room in an intense glow which mimicked and surpassed the strength of the natural sunlight that was still struggling valiantly to invade the room through the white slatted blinds.

From my vantage point seated on a large plump sofa, my surroundings did not look like a place of screams and torture, of blood splattered walls, or of bleached skeletons hanging from rusted hooks. Instead, the room was beautifully decorated with rich dark panels of wood rising from the skirting board to the height of a small child, followed by striped red and yellow paper with a velvety surface, running towards the ceiling all the way up to the height of two enormous bookcases which stood facing each other from opposite sides of the room. And where the paper ended, and about one metre below the ceiling, on all four walls, ran a carved wooden rail from which hung pictures of important people, including the familiar face of our Prime Minister Mr. Norman Manley, and HRH Elizabeth the Queen of England. And still in admiration Jamaica of the splendid decoration, I noted a centrally located and heavily tufted red and yellow rug on which stood the large dark brown oval shaped table at which the adults sat on three of the eight matching chairs - all smoothly upholstered in red and yellow striped satin fabric. In the far distance on either side of the French doors, stood two small identical tables, each bearing a table lamp of substantial size. Their lights, like the blazing sun outside, fought valiantly with the brilliance of the sparkly chandelier overhead, and in their battle for supremacy, seemed to have given up trying to light the large room and instead, in a fit of resignation, had thrown their weak yellow glow onto the shiny wooden floor beneath them. The repetition of the red and yellow colours of the fabric on the chairs and curtains tried to remind me of something against which my memory railed, but I did note that the armchair on which I sat, plus the two larger sofas and a further armchair, together with the set of floorlength curtains which covered the French windows at the far end of the room also matched the patterns on the walls.

Just as my observations ended, Mr. Roberts strolled over and knelt down beside me, clasped both of my small hands in his large soft and liberally freckle-decorated hands, then asked me in a soft kind voice 'Yu feeling all right Miss Cass?' I nodded, and he murmured 'Good, Good' while nodding his very large head. After a pause he said while looking deep into my eyes 'Your grandparents tell me that you had a fright todeh. Is that right?'

I suddenly remembered the purpose of why we were here. I swallowed hard as my chin lowered itself onto my chest, and a voice which sounded like someone else's, said 'Yes, there...

there was a…a bad man on the road'. I can now see the face of the man, and once more a nervous feeling, like a hot and enormous wave came over me while hot tears pricked the back of my eyes, and in spite of the coolness of the room, a dampness began to form on my forehead. Also not for the first time that day, I heard the loud 'lub dub' sound of my swiftly beating heart, heard my breathing as though from someone else, and felt the heat from my own small hands. It was then that my pacifier of sugar and water, the balm of all Jamaican children's woes, was placed in my hands – for the third time that day.

Mr Roberts began to speak in a soft but firm voice, deliberately separating each word with a pause while he patted the back of one of my hands in tune 'We-are-goingto-catch-that-bad-man-so-you-can-go-to-de-shap-for-your-sweets-wheneva-you-like.' The last three words were said with great emphasis.

He asked me again if I was 'All right?' then after glancing briefly over his shoulder he whispered in the voice of a school storyteller on the verge of revealing a secret, 'Miss Cass, some of my officers are going to come out and have a little chat with you. Is that all right with you?' I nodded, and he continued, 'They're going to ask you some questions, so I just want you to tell them the answers as clearly as you remember them. Can you do that for me Miss Cass?'

'Yes, I can' I said, 'What is de questions about?'

Automatically, like all grownups, he corrected my grammar and repeated my question

'What are the questions about?'

'Yes'

'Well Miss Cass,' and he leaned in until our foreheads were almost touching. 'We want to find out some more about the bad man, so we can catch him. We want to set a trap for him.' I decide that I would like the bad man to be caught in a trap while he is trying to run away. Looking up and into the distance, he said, 'Here comes my officers, Miss Cass. So, do your best, please.' Then he rose up slightly unsteadily, patted me on the head and walked off to re-join my grandparents.

I look over my shoulder to see an orderly line of policemen all dressed in regulation red and black uniforms, leisurely but determinedly strolling towards me. Their faces are nearly all familiar. I've seen them in the town and in other locations. On the streets near my school, from the windows of my church across the way, in the market with their families, and even sitting on their verandas in their everyday clothes smoking, and sometimes to my surprise, drinking beer. I slither silently from my chair and stand, just as I would in school whenever the headmaster entered our classroom.

Standing in a semi-circle formation, they smiled down at me, while one officer who had the widest smile asked,

'Awright Miss Cassie?' I nodded, and he patted me softly on my head. His hand then shifted to my shoulder and he said, 'We can ask yu some questions?' I stare up at him and nod. Then in one smooth movement and without warning, they, like practiced ballerinas, all knelt around me in a semi-circle. Entranced, I looked from left to right at their formation and note that with their brown faces level with mine they looked like children of my size, but with very big heads and hairy faces. As they stared back at me, the officer with the wide smile who knelt directly in front of me and who was the tallest and palest with unusual bright green eyes like a peacock's feathers, asked 'Miss, Cass, do you like school?'

'Yes' I answered.

'And you like your teachers?'

'Yes. Especially Mrs. Commen' I add.

'Oh, dat's nice. She's my aunty.' He continued 'So what subjects you like?'

I tell him that it's reading and writing and games, especially 'Row, row, row your boat'. Then, because he's a policeman and can give orders to other people, I think that he might be able to do something for me, so I share with him that I did not like sums. But he only nodded and gave me what I believe was a sympathetic smile. Another officer then took over and asked me if I was happy to be on holiday. I suddenly remembered, again, why we were at the station, and I began to feel a familiar prickly sensation building up behind my eyes. Quickly, the green eyed man nodded and said in a firm and friendly voice 'Yes, you will enjoy your holiday Miss Cass. Don't you doubt it" he added with feelings. Continuing with the same firm authority in his voice he said, 'After today we are going to catch that bad man who robbed you.' After glancing at the others he flashed me another big wide smile before saying in a low serious voice 'Cassie, please tell us what happened today.'

Once again, my heart began to drum as I recalled the events. In a shaky and high pitched voice I began, 'I saw...a bad man when...when I was going to the shop.' 'And then Mr. Bennett took me home' I added.

A swift glance passed between them before each officer, speaking in a soft voice, took turns from left to right to ask me questions.

'Have you ever seen that man before?' one asked

'No' I replied

'What did he look like?' asked another

I turned and looked deep into the speaker's eyes and said 'He was a black man'. The words sounded strange in my mouth. Strange and full of wonder because I had not spoken such words before. And not ever had I had to say 'a black man' before. A white sweetie man was our bogeyman. Not a black man.

'A black man?' asked the officer. And even his voice seemed to hold a note of surprise.

'Yes, he was a black man' I said again, as if once more trying to convince myself. To understand why we had not been taught to look out for a black Sweetie man.

'Black like me?' said the first man

I stared into his light coffee coloured face and decided.

'No.' I said looking around the semi-circle.

'No. Like that man' I said pointing to the very dark ebony coloured officer who knelt in the semi-circle.

'I see', he said after glancing to his left. All the other officers stared at their friend too.

'Where did you see the man, Cass?' asked another officer.

'He was sitting on the bridge. Near the Bowen's Road' I added.

'What did he look like?' asked another.

'He had a hard face' I said.

'Describe it please, Cassandra' said the first man again.

'It was like a big dog's bone. It was a boney face' I added.

'Not a fat face?' said another.

I turned and looked into his own face. No. It was a long boney face. Like this' I said, and sucked in my cheeks while I touched my cheekbones to emphasise the boniness of the man's face.

They smiled and nodded before one of the officers repeated my answer. 'A long boney face?' I nodded.

'Are you sure of that Cassandra?' he asked looking into my eyes.

'Yes,' I said with certainty, 'he had a long face.'

Then the main policeman spoke again. 'Which of us do you think have a face like that bad man Cassandra?'

I slowly studied their faces from one end of the semicircle to the other until I found one. It was a kind face but a long face.

'It was like his face' I said pointing to the last man on my right.

Slowly, and with what appeared to be caution, they all turned away from me and stared long and hard at their friend. I too looked at him and saw that he seemed to recoil as he in turn stared back at them. One officer asked me 'Miss Cass, did the robber have long plaits?'

'No' I answered.

'What was his hair like?'

'It was short.'

'Was his hair grey?'

'No, it was black'

'Are you sure, Cassie?' asked the main officer.

'Yes I am' I said, and I nodded.

I was sure, because the picture of the robber's face returned firmly behind my eyes. He sat there as I had seen him when I had turned the corner earlier in the day. The main man handed me my drink and said I was doing very well, and he wondered if they could ask me just a few more questions. I nodded, and they continued.

'So, what was he wearing, Cassandra?' asked the main man.

'Shorts' I replied.

'What sort of shorts?'

'Khaki shorts'

'What colour was it?'

'Light brown'

'What, like what the boys at your school wear?'

'Yes, like that', I smiled.

'And were they long shorts?'

'Yes. Down to his knees.'

'Was he wearing a shirt?' asked one officer

'Yes.'

'What kind?'

'A flowery shirt.'

'Can you describe it please?'

'Yes.'

'Go on Cassie', said the main man

'It was a big shirt. With short sleeves'

What colour was it?'

Again, I had gone to the picture stored fresh and new and sharp in my memory. 'It was yellow with big red flowers all over it.' A car hooted loudly in the Content Road and he repeated my answer. 'Yellow with big red flowers all over it?'

'Yes', I replied. And I can now see the bad man's shirt, his ash coloured arms and his long talon-like fingers with their jagged, yellowing nails. And the dirt embedded under each one giving them a stripy appearance. I shivered, and the main man handed me my drink again. And they watched me in silence as I took a long cool gulp.

Now the first officer asks me 'Did the man speak to you Cassie?'

Something inside me lurched as if I had done something wrong. Yes, it was my fault why the robber had been angry. Yes, I had made him cross by not following his instructions. By not doing what he had told me to do. I heard myself in a shaky halting voice say, 'He said...he said...he said, come here little girl' I stuttered. Now the main man seemed to be in charge again. He reached out and touched my arm before he asked me all of the questions that followed.

'And did you go to him?' Now I am back at the bridge and I hear his voice of command. And how his adult voice had triggered a response to obey.

The natural response of a Jamaican child who interacts with an adult. But still, I had felt a resistance against this strange sweetie man who wasn't a real sweetie man. How something unknown had reared up inside me at his request for me to 'Come here'. Something unknown and strong had resisted him and made me utter the difficult word 'No!' But then the word had created anger and danger and fear.

'I said 'No', I answered. I looked deep and enquiringly into the kind green eyes of the main man. He glanced at the officer beside him and then back at me before he said, 'Good Cassandra'. 'Good.' As if he had read my thoughts. Then he continued. 'Did he say anything else to you?'

'Yes.'

'What did he say?'

I looked over at my grandma and she nodded

'He said...he said, come here little girl or A going to cut off your neck' I heard their sharp intake of breath.

'Did he say that?' and I detected in his voice, a mixture of amazement and disbelief mixed with anger.

'Yes', I said.

'So, he said 'come here little girl or A going to chop off your neck?'

'No.' And I fought back the tears prickling under my eyelids. 'No, he said...he said, 'come here little girl or A going to cut off your neck' I corrected.

I now stared steadfastly at the blurred pattern of the flowery rug while I twisted and turned the cylinder of handkerchief in my hand. The green-eyed man placed his hand on my shoulder as he asked in a very soft voice. 'So, what did you do Cassie?'

Now again I saw myself walking stiffly over to the man. Saw my shoulders all hunched up as I listened for a noise in the silence. Of a car. A voice. Anything. Anyone. Just someone to rescue me and chase the monster away. Now I said. 'I went over to where he was sitting.'

I hung my head with the memory. Once more my pacifier was in front of me and I took a long deep slow gulp as the image of the new sweetie man materialised time and again in front of me. I felt his malevolent presence. And saw him staring at me, and even though I had not looked into his eyes I somehow felt threatened by them. And at my recollections of when he had waved me away, I again experienced a down pouring of relief as tears trickled down my face. Instantly, a forest of arms reached out to encircle me and pat me like gentle, soft waves on my head, my shoulders and my back, while the green eyed man dabbed my face with his own white handkerchief. The experience I had wanted as I had faced the robber. Then I watched as the choreographed dancers, rose, and moved away in single file in the direction from which they had appeared.

While my grandmother dabbed my face again, Mr Roberts patted me on the shoulder and says in a soft comforting voice that I've done well. Then 'Miss Cass, we will definitely catch that raa...' but he, like my grandfather earlier, stopped suddenly, before continuing 'We will definitely catch that bad man who troubled you today.' He knelt down beside me and showed me a big black book in which there was a lot of spidery joined-up writing. 'See Miss Cass, we have everything written down here.'

He turned the crisp noisy pages, and then without warning asked, 'And what do you think we goin to do with that bad man when we find him, Miss Cass?' I was about to say, 'Take back my money?' when he surprisingly answered his own question. 'We going to lock him up!' he said. 'Yes, he continues in a very upbeat tone, we going to lock him up and chow away the key. Believe me!'

He quickly unfurled himself to his full height before saying, in a voice full of rage and to no one in particular. 'God damn, I'm sick to death of lazy man in this country of ours feeling they can wander the streets an hole up and pick the pocket of every law abiding citizen'. He paused. 'That is bad enough, he said as he looked at my grandparents. But when dey start to pick the packit of children and threaten to kill dem? Dat is another matter!' 'They have to be stapped! Stapped once and for all!' he added fiercely. For a moment he didn't look like the Mr. Roberts who had bent down and looked into my eyes.

I had waited for a break in his monologue, to ask him why he was going to throw away the key but even when he paused I was reluctant to interrupt. He seemed oblivious of his audience as he again continued angrily, in a mixture of Jamaican and English words 'I'm fed up of it. And if dey tink dey going to get away wid it, dey have another ting coming.'

Then as if by magic, he produced a large white handkerchief into which he enveloped almost all of his face for a few seconds before emerging from it as if suddenly remembering that he was not alone. He stared at my grandad and said in a low, menacing and raspysounding voice 'Yes sir, we going to show dese dirty good for nothing scoundrels, who is the boss in this town.'

'I'm going to show dem who run tings round here! Show dem the real bad man!' he growled.

As we moved towards the exit, Mr. Roberts turned and spoke to my grandfather. 'Right Sam he said, This is the plan.'

His voice now fell to what he thought was a whisper, but I heard him say 'I'm going to be sending an officer out every day, starting today, to find this mad man.' He took a deep noisy breath before continuing 'To find him and bring him back here so I can deal with him.' He paused 'Yes, deal with him good and proper.'

My grandfather nodded enthusiastically, while my gran glanced down at me with a worried expression as Mr. Robert's voice began to rise again.

'I'll teach him to threaten children. I'll teach him a lesson he'll never forget. Yes Sir, when I finish wid im, he won't want to even walk near a likkle child again, much less look at one.'

I stared up at him and imagined him standing in the pulpit of the nearby church.

Now my grandmother, enjoying her umpteenth mango, breaks in on my thoughts, 'Everybody was pleased with de way you remembad everything about the robba.'

'Good.' I said. 'It's still clear in my memory.'

'Yes I'm sure ma darling. Roberts gave you a drawing book and some colouring pencils to draw anyting you remembad.' She paused, 'Dey did use some of your work to help them to catch the tief, you know. You did a lot of drawings about the

robbery, and of de man. Day and night.

She paused.

We couldn't stap you drawing.' and then continued *'One of the drawings yu did that we couldn't help laughing at though, was of a dawg in a cage using a spoon to eat his dinner. A doon't know where yu get dat fram.'*

Now my gran laughs out loud and I can't help joining her as I recall my fixation of wanting to know who occupied that cage that I had seen through a half-opened door at the police station.

As we leave, Mr Roberts thrust his massive head inside the car on my grandad's side and in a low ominous voice said 'Sam, I have to catch him soon.'

'Yes' replied my grandad in a low deep voice. 'Before the people get their hands on him first'.

I watch the headlights of our car slicing through the now empty blackness of the quiet Content Road. There is no one to be seen. I stare up at the black star-filled sky and listen to the howls of the invisible night creatures.

Following our visit to the police station, I played the role of the unseen listener and silently imbibed the daily bulletins of the adults. Everyone waited with bated breath for the capture of the bad man. Every stranger was viewed with suspicion and scrutinised. In most cases, according to unsubstantiated reports, they were questioned in less than polite tones and without preamble or niceties. After being eyed suspiciously, they would be asked in a bold fashion

'Weh yu come fram?'

'Yu bin here before?'

Others faced more intense scrutiny regarding the case

'Tell me, yu did hole up a likkle girl and treten to kill har?' before the person under suspicion scuttled swiftly out of town, thinking the questioner was a mad man.

Others were repeatedly asked for assurances that they were not the guilty party

'Yu sure is nat yu?'

This was usually followed up with a doubtful and threatening

'Me hope yu sure!'

Then there was the usual appeal to some strangers for help with the case 'Hey man, yu know whan smaddy who rab a likkle girl de adda day?'

This form of interrogation was often followed by a veiled warning to leave town as soon as possible 'So, when yu a leave?'

These visitors would also no doubt make a hasty exit from town before sundown.

Weekly updates on our veranda, over iced drinks, were also given by Mr Roberts. He said 'Sam, nat a week go by widout some sighting of a stranger fitting the description'. Every week, people who would never put a foot into a police station, fine dem way up the drive to come tell us dey si a strange man up in the hills.' He paused and dabbed his forehead which now had ridges in it. 'Or dey si one down in the bay. Or dey si somebody lounging suspiciously in a car, or on a bus, or sitting on a wall.' He shook his large head dolefully. 'Man,' he continued, in a low tired voice, 'de most dangarous move any man can mek in dis town dese days is to sit down on a wall far a res. But most a de people who go against all their natural fear of de police and come in, is to tell us dat they si stranger a hang round a shap where dey children playing.' Then after a deep sigh he said 'Yey mon, A could fill a book wid what's going on'.

All rumours he reassured them, were always investigated, and all strangers when spotted by the police, were always, he added, questioned; before being unofficially driven out of town by concerned citizens. But so far, he reported in a sad tone, none had been arrested or convicted. And as regards the policeman sent out on his daily bicycle rides, success had not come his way. Although he had acted on tipoffs from concerned residents about suspicious strangers, he had never been lucky enough to find them waiting to be interviewed, and maybe arrested on his return the following day. It was at one of these reporting occasion that my gran, sitting silently throughout, had made the suggestions about asking for help from Kingston, the capital. And following her intervention, the first of many hurried visits to the police station for the identification of the bad man was made.

As with all future alerts it began with the silence of our surroundings being abruptly broken by a surreal dreamlike pleadings of a distant voice from the Gale Road. It wafted up through the densely packed and dark banana walk, rushed around the bend of the long L-shaped drive and finally after coalescing with the raucous barking of our dogs, landed onto the veranda where we sat as usual, engaged in a mixture of dozing and reading. Above the perpetual hum of crickets, bird song and the gentle background swish of the breeze in the trees, the desperate and repetitive voice had cried 'Please hole de dawg'. 'Please hole de dawg'. And in response, after each surreal wail, my grandfather, or grandmother, or both, (with muted interjections from me) would muster all their energies and shout back 'Come up!' 'Come up!' After which, a boy would come bursting around the corner of the drive like a suddenly released branch.

On the first occasion, the messenger - or human 'police telephone' as my grandmother referred to him and all the others who over time followed - ran up towards the house looking frantically from left to right, no doubt searching for the bad dogs indicated on the sign at the entrance of the property. In between gasps he said that he had a message 'fram de,' and he bent to rest his hands on his knees, 'police station.' And while my grandmother poured him a drink of water he continued, 'Mr. Rabert said' pant pant 'could you come now', pant pant pant 'to identify de tief'.

While he desperately gulped his drink, my grandparents grabbed their hats, I changed into my church shoes, and we all rushed down the steps, piled into the car, boy and all, and drove swiftly away to the police station.

On this first interrogative visit, I made an amazing discovery. There in the cage, I had seen not an animal bristling with anger at being confined, but a man, standing forlornly, the knife and fork, recently used, laying at his unshod feet. Fear was banished and replaced at the sight, by something I could not recall ever feeling before. It was an emotion I later learnt was called pity, and out of which came unspoken questions like newly unfurled buds. I had scrutinised the confined man standing with the cutlery at his feet while he stared with terrified eyes at my grandparents. Then Mr Roberts had directed him to look at me. And completely taken by surprise at my presence, he had looked down with amazement clearly written in his eyes. I had stared quizzically up at him while everyone else had stared optimistically down at me. And to Mr. Roberts' question of 'Is this the man Miss Cass?' my answer was 'No, Mr Roberts' while the reasons spun inside my head - No, not dark enough. Face not boney enough. And definitely the wrong kind of fingers, as well as the wrong kind of voice. Too soft. Not frightening at all when he had been directed by Mr. Roberts to tell me his full name.

So, weeks had turned into months and years as the lone policeman repeated his daily fruitless journeys on his ancient creaking bicycle over the white gravel strewn Gale Road. My chuckling grandmother had commented on one occasion when the tell-tale creaking wafted up through the coconut trees and into the garden, that the bike was 'tirsty for a dose of eyel'. And as his daily routine was never impeded by inclement weather or the onset of changing seasons, he had, day after day, doggedly and slowly trawled the country lanes, looking for the man whom only I had seen. The man whom, according to angry and anxious parents, he had just missed. But for the benefit and assurance of my grandparents and the neighbourhood, Mr. Roberts had kept him on his prolonged quest. In fact, this upholder of law and order kept to such a strict timetable that more than once I had heard my grandmother bafflingly say, 'Lawd, A could set mi watch by him', as each day the sound of his bicycle reminded us that a dangerous man was still on the loose. Somewhere. Anywhere.

In the meantime, my descriptions and some of my drawings of the bad man were circulated, with one, according to Mr. Roberts being placed in the National Gleaner. 'Even non-readers will know the word 'Wanted' he had said as he sat on our veranda one Sunday afternoon flourishing the poster embellished by my handiwork which depicted a boney faced character wearing a flowery shirt and sporting frighteningly long discoloured talons wrestling with a starched lace-trimmed handkerchief.

'Almost as good as a photograph!' he had added laughing triumphantly, as he had looked down at me, before continuing in a pensive voice while staring at the poster 'A dealing with a slippery customer'.

Quickly, visions invaded my mind and caused me to wonder how the bad man's slipperiness had been discovered. What confrontations I wondered had taken place to familiarise him with the oiliness of the thief but had prevented him from maintaining his grip. Who I wondered had oiled him and caused him to slip out of Mr. Roberts' grasp? And had he encountered him at the spot where I had seen him? Well, whatever he felt like, his escape had affected our freedom. Because now, children were forced to travel the long way round to the shop, and worse, all little girls had to walk with a big boy. Groups of friends shared stories of the constant bloodcurdling warnings from parents about dawdling and gazing, and about not stopping along the way to show-off complicated time-consuming dance moves, or the playing of turn-taking elasticated and never ending hopscotch games hurriedly drawn on hot asphalt. Errands became a joyless chore.

'Yes,' said my gran, 'It was some months after the robbery that Errol your cousin came to live with us. His mother was sick and couldn't look afta him so I had to have him here. Dat was a godsend. A didn't have to worry so much every time yu was out of my sight, even fo one minute. It was a constant worry.'

Now I ask her why she had asked me about the man, and I waited quietly for her untold story. Adopting her informal home-use-only language, she began

'My dear yu soun like English woman, eeh?' Then in a voice that has all her vowels tumbling over each other, she mimics me, which in turn makes me chuckle.

But I persist in my question about the bad man

'Go on grandma. Why do you ask?'

She stops eating, looks directly into my face, and says

'I wasn't going to bother telling you since you still so upset about de whole thing' she said

'Go on gran. I can handle it'

She looks deep into my eyes and say, 'The police caught him you know.'

I am speechless.

'Yes' she says, Caught him soon after you went to England.'

'They did?' a feeling of relief sweeps over me. 'That is amazing!' I silently congratulate my younger self for my accurate descriptions as once more I see his bone-like face, his skin colour, body type, clothes, and the claw-like hands.

'Got him!' I said aloud, triumphantly.

'Yes, dey did get him' continues my grandma in a low but equally triumphant tone. 'Caught de brute'

'So how did they find him, gran?'

'Well it look as if he thought everybody forgot about it so he was boasting and tole a friend. Look like de friend wasn't too happy with what he had done to you, and from the sound of tings, to a few others over the years. So his fren give him up to the police.'

'Serves him right!' I said.

'Plenty of good people around us you know, Cass.'

'Yes gran. You're right.' And we continued to eat our delicacies, enveloped in a self- satisfied silence.

Then I remembered. 'I didn't look at him when I was near him you know grandma.' I only looked at him when I turned the corner before the bridge'.

Pausing in the gentle demolition of her snack, she studies me with an expression bordering on adoration and said 'Well, I sure glad he didn't see you looking at him mi dear' And she continues 'Maybe dat's what saved mi little Cassie's life.'

She looks down at something invisible on the ground, shakes her head ruefully and says with feelings 'God knows.'

She shivers involuntarily as though from a passing cold breeze that only she can detect. But watching her, I get the impression that there is more to come. So, I wait. 'Well' she continued cautiously 'They did send him to prison, but...'

'Come on gran, spit it out' I say.

She smiles and with a chuckle, repeats what I have just said to her; once more filling her mouth with English vowels. We laugh together at her language gymnastics and the mood lifts slightly as we fall about enjoying the phrase. 'Well, she repeats, Dey did send im to prison.'

'Yes! And I hope he stays there and rot.' I add.

'Cassandra, listen.' She says softly, touching my arm. 'No grandma, I respond, I know you believe in forgiveness and I do too, but he threatened to cut off my neck.'

And I remembered and repeat the words of Mr. Roberts.

'I hope they threw the key away where no one would ever find it'.

She looks at me with a rueful expression and seemed reluctant to go on. As if she too longed to forget. But my old habit of pressing her for answers hadn't diminished and I held her gaze for more. 'So, did he die there then gran?'

We had started, and we had to finish. I needed to know how the story ended.

'No,' she continued, almost apologetically. 'He didn't die in prison.'

'Is he still ...?'

'No' she interrupts, 'He spent some years in prison for what *he did.' And after a pause, 'But he came out.'*

'And?' I ask almost hesitantly. I began to doubt that this story had a happy ending. 'Tell me grandma. What has he done?'

'Well', she continued, 'After being out of prison for some years he got a job'

'A job? As what?'

'Well....' She began, studying the red terracotta floor tiles as if she was seeing them for the first time.

I waited.

'Well you won't believe this Cass.'

'What granma?' I ask, almost afraid to hear her answer.

'Well, he got a job in Kingston' She paused.

I wait and then almost reluctantly, ask her 'As what grandma?'

She said 'As a police officer, Cass'. And she looks at me with sadness in her eyes.

I'm speechless as I in turn stare back at her.

Then in a voice laden with sorrow and what sounds like fear, she continues 'Then later they made him the Chief of Police'

We both stare silently into the distance at the bend in the L shaped drive. And I see the little girl racked with terror standing in front of the Sweetie Man wearing his disguise...

The End

Coming soon...

'More Jamaican Childhood Stories!'

Teaching Packs

Hidden Histories

Made in the USA
Columbia, SC
11 September 2018